INTUITION &
PSYCHIC
ABILITY

YOUR SPIRITUAL GPS

Jennifer O'Neill

Published by:

 Limitless Publishing, LLC
Kailua, HI 96734
www.limitlesspublishing.com

First Print Edition: August 2012
ISBN-13: 978-0615685090 (Limitless Publishing, LLC)
ISBN-10: 0615685099

Cover and interior design by Streetlight Graphics.

Information provided in this material should not be relied upon as a substitute for advice, programs, or treatment that you would normally receive from a licensed professional, such as a lawyer, doctor, psychiatrist, financial adviser, or any other licensed professional.

Table of Contents

What is Psychic Ability?

I have been teaching people about intuition and psychic ability for many, many years. What a fascinating subject! I find it quite amazing how the very topic of psychic ability provokes such a strong response, or opinion, from people. In my experience, when you bring up the subject of psychic ability, it intrigues some people, while really annoying others, who refer to it as, "Impossible and ridiculous!"

So what is psychic ability exactly?

Psychic ability refers to an *extrasensory perception* (commonly referred to as ESP), which is the ability to receive information with the mind, which is not gained through your physical senses.

To many people, it's quite baffling! How do you receive information without using your physical senses? How is that possible? We use our physical senses to gain knowledge for everything; we use them to make sense of the world around us. Scientists have been studying this phenomenon for years, trying to figure it out. They run experiments and tests on various subjects, measuring brain wave patterns and heart rate, all in the hopes of getting some answers on how psychic ability is possible. Who can blame them? They are scientists, that's what they do. However, they're missing something, which is very important to understanding psychic ability.

Psychic ability, and your psychic senses, are not one of your physical senses, but one of your spiritual senses.

It's the ability to tap into your spiritual body, and the ability to utilize one of your spiritual senses, in order to retain information. This is what trips people up. Many scientists, who are trying to make sense of how this phenomenon works, or how it can even be possible, *are only studying the physical body*. This makes perfect sense to them, as they are usually very grounded in their own physical existence. The mistake being made here is they don't take into consideration the spiritual body. They miss this important piece of information because, in the rare instance they are even aware of the spiritual body, it is very unlikely they will understand how the spiritual body works. However, in most instances, it's safe to say they don't even know what the spiritual body is.

Here's why this is so important. Imagine for a minute that someone from 5,000 years ago was transported into our current time. (Yeah, I know, just bear with me here, it's an analogy). Anyway, this person has absolutely no knowledge whatsoever about electricity. They don't know what it is, they don't even know it exists, yet every time they push a button on this square we call a television, something miraculous happens. A flash of light beams, and color begins to take form in the shape of pictures. They clearly begin to hear people talking. They know that through this little box they are seeing pictures and hearing things, they know other people are seeing and hearing the same things, but they can't understand how this information is coming through this little device! They're so fascinated by this little device that they decide they want to take it with them, so they take the television outside, but it doesn't work. They bring it back in, and set it up in the same manner, and it works again. "Hmmm, must have something to do with this string or cord attached to the television," they think to themselves, "but how does this cord thing work?" They spend years trying to figure out what makes the television activate with the push of a button. Meanwhile, this person also has no knowledge of satellites, television waves or cameras. So even if they do finally figure out how the television is powered (with electricity), they will then want to know how this information gets to this little box.

You see, many scientists are trying to figure out psychic ability in the same manner, by studying the end result first. They're trying to figure out how the process works by monitoring the physical body; while it's translating the information it receives. They're starting too late in the process. You can't understand how something works (in this case receiving information without gaining knowledge through the physical senses), without first understanding the process that takes place in order to produce that end result (the process of utilizing the spiritual body and tapping into spiritual resources). They're going about it backwards.

No one will ever be able to fully grasp the concept, or fully understand psychic ability, while only looking for answers with the physical body; it isn't possible. What they will discover, however, is how your physical body translates the information it receives from your spiritual senses into the physical realm. These things will show up on heart monitors, on brain wave patterns, etcetera. When it comes to psychic ability and psychic senses, there is such an argument about having "enough substantial proof" in order to prove its validity in the scientific community, that people are not quite sure what to make of the whole thing. We currently live in a time where people are so grounded into the physical realm that they rely heavily on physical evidence in order to "believe" in something. The funny thing is, do you know what a belief actually is?

Belief means that you "believe" there will be a certain outcome in the future; which may or may not be realistic, without substantial proof!

Look it up! I find it very odd, yet interesting, how much it sounds like the definition for psychic ability. People take great pride in their beliefs, realistic or not, even without substantial proof. Believing in something that's widely accepted, people who consider themselves to have a strong belief system are even regarded as noble, or highly respected, for taking a strong stance or position for something they believe in. Some people will "believe" a scientist or a skeptic's personal "beliefs" on psychic ability, and disregard their own experiences as not valid, or impossible, because they assume these people have more knowledge then they do on the subject. Crazy, isn't it? What makes this subject even more fascinating is the fact that everyone has this ability, scientists and skeptics alike, they just spend a lifetime trying to convince themselves and others that it isn't possible. Skeptics have taken the position of, "I don't have it. Nobody has it, because it doesn't exist!" Can you deny that you have it? Sure. Can you ignore its existence? Of course, knock yourself out! But doing these things will not change the reality of its existence.

But it hasn't always been this way ...

Throughout history, on every continent in the world, psychic ability and the spirit world has been regarded as a very important component to our physical existence. It has been embraced and often utilized effectively, dating back hundreds to even thousands of years. There has been recorded evidence of strong beliefs in things such as the spirit world, the afterlife, psychic ability, and astrology in almost all cultures at one time or another. It was a different time, however; a time when people very much embraced their spiritual body as a large part of their existence. They felt strongly they were only here in the physical realm temporarily; however, the essence of who they were lay within their spiritual body. In fact, these things were taken quite seriously in most cultures during times dating back to most of BCE and in the early years of AD. It is no secret how strongly the Egyptians believed in the spiritual body and prepared for their own spiritual body's journey into the afterlife. Buddhism dates back to 6th century BCE in which the spiritual body is a part of their belief system, even to this day. There were Oracles in Greece, which date back to 8th century BCE. Oracles were a priest or priestess (more commonly it was a priestess, or a woman), acting as a medium or source, who was believed to be receiving information from the Gods. Many times they would speak in tongues, which needed to be translated by a priest. The practice of going to see the Oracle in hopes of receiving information from the Gods started around 8th century BCE and the last recorded response was given in 393 AD. People would travel for many, many miles to receive a prediction from the Oracle, including the affluent, heads of state, and the common folk. Pythia, most commonly known as the Oracle of Delphi, was a well-known priestess during this time. The people had such faith in her that no major decision was made without her prediction or guidance. She provided guidance to the many Kings of the time regarding war and battle.

Around the world, it has been recorded throughout history that Kings would consult psychics and astrologers before making any major decisions. Kings, heads of state, even presidents, would utilize their abilities in order to help them decide when to go into battle or war, on how to prepare themselves, help them calculate the most favorable timing to do so, and what the probable outcome would be. Astrologers and psychics would also offer their guidance on when to plant crops, as well as probable invasions. They were commonly referred to as the "seers" or "seer of God." They were often part of any king's court or council. Psychic ability, the spirit world, and the afterlife were very much respected as part of everyday living in many cultures, up until the more recent times.

As we have come into current times, we now live in a time where people are very unaware of their spiritual body and spiritual self, so they are far more inclined to believe that physical existence is the only existence. And because of the way in which the psychic process works, *a prediction of future events or the outcome of future events without any substantial "physical" proof,* it is very hard to prove in the physical realm, therefore, it is just speculation as far as many people are concerned.

Since there is no way to prove such outcomes, apart from monitoring success rate after the fact, scientists have been struggling with the validity of psychic ability for years. How does a person predict future events without any substantial proof of a certain outcome, or without any previous knowledge? It's fascinating! It's also mind-boggling for anyone who is unaware of the spiritual body, or to someone who needs "substantial physical proof" of how it may be possible.

Psychic ability is just as much a part of your existence as is your kidneys and your heart. Just because you cannot see them, does not mean these things do not exist. (Granted you have proof now, as they have been shown to you on x-rays and diagrams, but at some point in history, how did anyone even know they existed?) These organs of yours are in full operation, everyday, doing what they can, to help you live a good life. You could ignore them, however, ignore their existence and brush off any signals they give you. Brush off any aches, pains, or shortness of breath. In fact, many people do. If you choose this route, however, you will most certainly suffer some consequences that usually manifest themselves into physical problems. Your quality of life will certainly be affected.

Let me repeat that.

If you ignore a part of yourself that is doing what it can to help you live the best life possible, your quality of life will certainly be affected!

What is Intuition?

We have talked a lot about psychic ability, but what about intuition? What is intuition? How does intuition fit into the picture? People are often unsure of the difference between intuition and psychic ability.

Intuition is an *extrasensory perception* or a "knowing" of something you should or shouldn't do, without any substantial proof, which is accompanied by a noticeable feeling in the body.

Intuition is actually psychic ability, in an adolescent stage. In other words, it is psychic ability, which is developed to a lesser degree. They are essentially the same thing, just developed to different degrees. That being said, intuition is also the ability to receive information, which is not gained through your physical senses. However, pictures or images do not usually accompany intuition. It is a strong "sixth sense" feeling, which is trying to guide you in a particular direction. It usually comes in the form of a brief thought, but that thought is accompanied by "a feeling" felt in the body, which leads you to believe you should or shouldn't do something. Because of the way in which the intuition process works, and because it is a bit more subtle than the way psychic ability works, it is much easier, in many instances, for people to shrug it off as a random thought.

Intuition is not just a thought but a general overall "feeling" or strong sense felt in the body. This feeling can usually be felt in the chest or the stomach area, and it seems to represent or anticipate a certain outcome. The most common physical sensation, which people attribute to intuition, is what many refer to as a "gut feeling."

People often wonder about intuition, even their own intuition, since it seems to be a bit more realistic, or possible, and "socially acceptable." Why? Because everyone you know has probably experienced having had a "gut feeling" themselves, at least one time in his or her life. In fact, I personally have yet to run into anyone who has never experienced a gut feeling. (And yes, I am taking a poll!) Since many people have experienced this gut feeling themselves, or know someone who has, this seems to be enough substantial proof that intuition does indeed exist. Even though intuition is more widely accepted, it is often ignored.

Even when aware of its existence, people often don't pay much attention to their own intuition until they go against it. Then they say to themselves, "I knew I shouldn't have done that! I just had a feeling!" Intuition isn't complicated, it's very simple. The problem with intuition is that many times, since this guidance usually tends to pop into your head as a brief thought, people think their own mind is playing tricks on them, or being unreasonable. Here are a couple of stories about people who went against their own intuition.

Let's take Heather, for instance. Heather was an intelligent young girl, age 22, who was well aware of her own intuition. However, on one particular occasion she tried her best to justify this horrible feeling that was about to come over her. While returning from a relaxing vacation in Mexico with her boyfriend, their flight had a short layover in Houston, Texas. During this layover Heather began to get a horrible feeling in the pit of her stomach. She recognized this feeling right away, as it was similar to other intuitive feelings she had experienced in the past. This worried her. She told her boyfriend, "I don't think we should get on this flight, I think we should take another one." He asked why. "I just have a horrible feeling, I think we should change flights." Steve didn't want to pay the extra $100 to switch flights on a "feeling" Heather had, what sense did that make? He did his best to convince her that everything would be fine. So she agreed.

Soon the airline announced, "There is going to be a small delay, we will be boarding shortly." Heather began to feel even more uneasy. Steve was now getting annoyed and said she was being silly.

After an hour or so, the airline announced, "You can begin boarding now." Heather got up and with every fiber of her being telling her to turn around ... she boarded the airplane. She wrung her hands nervously and looked out the window, trying to distract herself. *I feel like I'm going to throw up,* she thought.

Steve grabbed her hand and squeezed it with a smile and said, "Stop worrying, it will be fine."

The plane taxied down the runway and took off without incident. Everything seemed fine at first, not much turbulence, and clear skies. Heather's mind tried to calm her nerves as she stared out the window, but it wasn't working.

About twenty minutes into the flight, there was suddenly a very loud pop. The noise was so startling; everyone immediately took notice and looked around to see what had happened as their hearts began to race. Suddenly, smoke began to fill the passenger cabin of the airplane. The plane had blown an engine! The captain immediately came over the loudspeaker and announced to the passengers, "Everybody stay calm and make sure your seatbelts are fastened. We've blown an engine and we are going to have to make an emergency landing." Since the landing needed to be immediate, the passengers were further instructed by the pilot. "Put your head between your legs as far as possible, as we are going to be experiencing a loss of cabin pressure," he said firmly. The plane made a steep dive then leveled out to make the emergency landing. The passengers were terrified, worried they would blow the other engine or not make it to the ground safely. Everyone was panic-stricken! Once they were on the ground safely, Heather made a vow never to go against her intuition again, and Steve made a vow to always listen to her.

The next story I have is about Bailey. Bailey was nineteen at the time of this incident; she had just graduated high school and was working at a radio station near her home. It was a Saturday morning when Bailey woke up and came down stairs to get some toast. On her way to the kitchen, she noticed her bird had died. The bird was not but a few months old, and had shown no signs of being sick, or unusual behavior. *Very strange*, she thought. Bailey had many animals at home, and they had always lived for a very long time.

After breakfast, while sitting at the kitchen table, her mother said to her, "I don't think you should go out tonight." Bailey asked why not. Her mother, who never talked to Bailey about her own intuition said, "I just think you should stay home tonight."

To most people, someone telling you or asking you not to do something you were planning on doing without a reasonable explanation, is not enough to make you change your plans. Needless to say, your mother telling you to stay home at the ripe old age of nineteen is most definitely not a reason for you to change your plans. So off she went to get ready for her day.

After leaving the house, Bailey's next stop was to pick up her paycheck from the radio station. When she got there, her paycheck was totally messed up. Friends were waiting on her to pick them up, but this was something that couldn't wait, the paycheck needed to be fixed right then and there. These things, coupled with Mom's advice to stay in for the night, began to give Bailey a weird feeling that maybe something was telling her to stay home. However, this weird feeling was not enough to make her change plans. She called her friends, told them she was going to be delayed, but she'd be there soon. Bailey couldn't help but think, *From the moment I got up, this day has not felt right.* But she continued on as planned. A few hours later with friends in tow, Bailey was heading out on the town, when suddenly … her car died. It was about two a.m and she tried to pull over, but the car was completely dead, so it needed to be pushed. Luckily, there was another car behind her with a few more friends. They got out, and decided to push the car off the side of the road while Bailey steered. Up ahead they noticed some headlights coming towards them in the distance. These headlights were bright, and seemed to be moving too much from side to side. The headlights were approaching fast, too fast to get out of the way. When Bailey noticed what was happening, the first thing she could think of was to slam her foot down on the brakes, in hopes of stopping her car from going backwards into her friends behind her in case she was hit.

Bailey was hit by a drunk driver that night. She was very lucky to be alive, but did not escape without injury. Because of her quick thinking, however, her friends escaped unharmed. Bailey is fully recovered now, and it was an event that changed her life forever. Not only did she decide to pay more attention to her own intuition, but she wanted to learn more about it and how to help other people in the process. Bailey is currently working full time as a healer.

Now granted these are two rather extreme stories on what can happen if you don't follow your own intuition. Don't be afraid. In both cases, looking back, these girls said had they listened to their intuition, they could have avoided putting themselves in those situations. It was one of those, "I knew I should've paid more attention to that feeling I had," moments. In other words, the intuition was not subtle in these cases, just ignored. Sometimes ignoring your intuition can result in getting a flat tire, or having an unpleasant experience, with nothing too life shattering.

Your intuition is a very good guidance system when listened to, which can help keep you out of harm's way.

Take Lisa, for instance. Lisa was a very hard worker at a very young age. She worked in the city at a local video store. It was a night job, something she did to earn extra income while going to college. One morning when she got up, she thought about what she had to do before going to work that night at six. Something immediately caught her attention, however. Every time she thought of going to work, she had a very bad feeling. Her stomach didn't feel good. Lisa never called out of work; in fact, she often worked while not feeling well. She prided herself on being a loyal and responsible employee. But all day this nagging feeling in the pit of her stomach wouldn't go away. She did other things to forget about it. She even tried to make sense of it by thinking, *Am I sick? Is there something that I'm missing?* But nothing came to mind, and it was different than a flu-like feeling. Lisa tried to wait it out as long as she could to see if it would go away, but it just got more intense. She recognized the feeling and worried that something might happen if she ignored it; she called out of work.

That night the video store was robbed at gunpoint, during the shift that Lisa worked. No one was injured, but she was grateful she hadn't been there.

Your intuition is meant to be used as guidance in time of need.

Ed and his daughter, Sophie, decided to take a road trip to visit relatives and attend a cousin's wedding in Michigan. Ed worked at the post office; he was in his mid to late 40s. Sophie was a student, around 24 years old at the time. They were both excited to spend some quality time together and see family. After driving for twelve hours, they could see their destination approaching. Since he'd only been to Michigan one time in his life, Ed was unfamiliar with the area. So he turned to his daughter and said, "Grab the directions so we know where we should go from here."

Sophie said, "Sure, where are they?"

"You don't have them?"

"No, I thought you grabbed them."

Realizing that neither of them had grabbed the directions and knowing they had no idea where they were going, they decided they better find a pay phone. It was around two a.m. in the morning by this time, so they were both exhausted, but they managed to find a phone booth. Looking through the phone book, they discovered the house they were looking for, Ed's sister's house, wasn't listed. They decided to call back home to get the address. After what seemed like an eternity, he turned to his daughter and said, "No answer. Everyone must be sleeping." They got back in the car and Ed said, "Okay, looks like we're on our own." Thoroughly exhausted, and having relied on his intuition in the past, he said to Sophie, "We're going to follow our instincts."

Sophie looked puzzled, "Sure, Dad," without much confidence. "Whatever you say."

"All right, car, we're looking for Margaret's house. Lead the way." Ed headed towards the highway and continued on in the same direction. They drove until he felt the urge to turn. "This is beginning to feel right to me." The exit took them into a neighborhood filled with rows and rows of houses. They both looked at the houses around them. Ed continued on through the neighborhood until he felt like something was telling him to slow down. "I think that might be my sister's house, right ..." as he pointed his finger towards the house, "... there."

Sophie's eyes widened in disbelief. It was three a.m. at this point, and right in that instant, the living room light turned on. Standing in the living room, they could see Margaret stretching, through the window. *Wow*, Sophie thought to herself, *how did that happen?*

When talking to Margaret about what happened, they asked what made her get up and turn the light on so late. She said that she just had the "urge" to go into the living room and turn the light on, so she did.

Even though many people refer to it as a "gut" feeling, it's important to understand this feeling is not always in the gut area. Sometimes it's felt in the chest, stomach or solar plexus area.

To help explain intuition a little bit further, I have made a list questions people often wonder about. Questions that I feel it helps to know the answers to in order to utilize your intuition most affectively.

What does intuition feel like?

Intuition feels like a thought. Only this thought is accompanied by a noticeable feeling in the body, for instance:

- Gut feeling
- Urge
- Strange feeling in chest, stomach or solar plexus area
- Stomachache
- Weird feeling in pit of the stomach

How will I be able to tell the difference between my own thoughts and intuition?

This is a very common question and one that really throws people off. It is actually not that hard:

1) These "thoughts" usually pop into your head out of nowhere. Your own thoughts are usually a chain of thoughts, which led you to what you are thinking at that moment in time. One thought leads to another, then another, and then another. Intuition usually feels more like you just had a random thought.

2) *Your own thoughts are not usually followed "simultaneously" by a noticeable feeling in the body.* When you have a thought, it usually takes a minute or two for your emotions to kick in and for you to have a reaction to the thought you were just thinking.

3) These thoughts tend to pop up when you're trying to figure out a solution to something, when there is probable danger involved, or when you're in need of guidance.

How do I know the difference between this "noticeable feeling in the body" and the flu or just my regular emotions?

1) *Regular emotions can be described very easily.* You can put your finger on it, such as: panic, excitement, happiness or sadness.

2) *Intuitive feelings are hard to describe.* You can't quite put your finger on it, so you'll find yourself thinking things like, "It makes no sense, but I just have a feeling to …" or "It just doesn't feel right," or "Something feels off, not right, or weird," and "I'm not sure why, but it feels right, or feels like the right thing to do."

3) *This feeling is more like a very strong sense of guidance.* Don't get too caught up in the details, it will either feel good to you or not so good. If this thought is accompanied by a good feeling, then your intuition is trying to guide you towards that direction. If the thought is accompanied by a not so good feeling, then your intuition is trying to steer you away from making that choice.

Intuition Exercise

I have a very good exercise that I'd like you to try at this time. This is a really great exercise that I use to teach to my clients, so they can learn how to use their own intuition. It also allows you to experience what your own intuition feels like. Once you experience that feeling, and understand what it is, it becomes hard not to recognize it whenever it pops up in the future.

1) Find a comfortable place, in which you will not be disturbed.

Preferably sitting in a chair in an upright position. Relax your body.

2) Next, I want you to think of something you have been struggling with making a decision on.

Something in which you are just unsure about what to do. It could be something like:

- Should I switch jobs?
- Should I move?
- Should I stay in this relationship?
- Should I buy a new car?
- Should I go back to work?
- Should I put my child in daycare?

You get the idea. Think of a question, and for the sake of this exercise I'm going to use the question, "should I move." (I get that question a lot.) Usually I'll walk my clients through this exercise before I give them my psychic opinion. Why? Because I want my clients to learn how helpful and reliable their own intuition is. To my client's surprise, their own intuition and my answer matches 99.99% of the time. When it is off just by a tiny bit, it's usually because the client immediately tries to justify their intuition with their mind and its logic right away ... explaining away their own intuition.

3) You're going to imagine two different scenarios.

One scenario in which you make a choice one way, and a second scenario in which you do the complete opposite. Since we are going to use the "should I move" issue as an example, in one scenario I will walk you through moving and the other scenario will be to stay where you are.

4) Next, I want you to close your eyes.

You cannot do this exercise with your eyes open. This is because when you have your eyes closed, your mind is forced to pay attention to how the body feels, and it begins to tune itself in naturally, harmonizing the physical body, the spiritual body, and your intuition. (Your eyes do not always have to be closed for your intuition to kick in, but when you're focusing on getting clarity on a particular issue, it's important that they are.)

5) Imagine the first scenario.

With your eyes closed, imagine that it's now six months later. Imagine you have stayed exactly where you are. You have not moved, nothing much has changed. Imagine that you're in the same routine day after day, probably working in the same job. How does that feel in the body? Really take notice. Does it feel good, bad, or indifferent? Don't try to analyze it, just notice the feeling.

6) Imagine the second scenario.

Imagine that it's six months later, you have moved and are in a new place. Imagine you are now in a new job. You've been working that job for a while, so you're now in a routine there. Imagine you have met new people and you don't see other people as much anymore. How does it feel to you? How does it feel in the body?

7) You will have a clear feeling of one feeling noticeably better than the other.

Think back to both scenarios; one always feels better than the other. It may not be by a landslide, although it's usually a significantly better feeling one way versus the other. However, don't discount it if one way only subtly feels better. That will be the way in which your intuition is trying to guide you.

8) Open your eyes.

You should have a sense of clarity at this point.

This exercise can be used with anything and it should be. It will help you tune your body with your own intuition and guidance system. You can do it with almost anything, staying in a relationship or not, going back to school or not, buying those new tires you need or not.

Your Spiritual Body & Psychic Ability

What is the spiritual body? Your spiritual body is similar to your physical body only in energy form. It is contains your Soul DNA or spiritual genetic system and the essence of who you are. It is you in your natural state.

Your spiritual body brings your physical body to "life."

Without your spiritual body, it is not possible for you to exist in the physical world. When you are born, your spiritual body enters and connects itself to your physical body through energy centers. These energy centers are what people refer to as your Chakras or Chakra System. When the two bodies merge together your physical body is given "life." Your physical body would be "lifeless" without your spiritual body. I'm sure many of you have experienced this lifeless feeling when you've been around a loved one who has left the physical plane. You can no longer feel them. It's weird to many, especially since your loved one visually looks the same, however, they don't feel the same. Your spiritual body is the power which allows your physical body to function. Without it, your physical body would be like a car with no battery. It has all of the physical components to go, but nothing to give it life.

Just like your physical body, your spiritual body has its own unique set of senses, a communication system, and a large energy center, which can be referred to as your energetic brain. Just as your physical brain works to gather and process knowledge on the physical plane, your spiritual body has its own energetic brain, which is located near the sixth and seventh chakras. It is dedicated to gathering knowledge and translating the information that it receives.

When developing and utilizing your intuition or psychic ability, you begin to synchronize your two bodies. The more developed and advanced you become is dependent on how well you learn to harmonize your spiritual and physical bodies in order to gather information needed at that time. In order to advance to the best of your ability, there is a hurdle which you must conquer.

You must find trust.

Trust within your whole being that your spiritual body is gathering information, which is valid and needed at that time. Gathering information in a way which you may not understand and most likely will not be backed up by physical proof.

In order to help you find this trust within yourself, it helps if you can understand the process in which this works.

Understanding the process

When working with your spiritual body and your psychic senses, the prediction of future events or the outcome of future events, *is usually done without any substantial proof.* Although the process itself, is really fairly simple, and it involves four basic steps.

This ability is a process:

1) It involves tapping into your spiritual body.

First, it involves tapping into your spiritual body in order to activate your psychic senses. This is a natural ability. However, if you have blocked it over the years, it may be an area in which you need to retrain yourself. This can be done through exercises. It also helps to understand what it "feels" like when you do utilize the spiritual body, and we will cover both in this book.

2) Gathering information from spiritual resources.

Your spiritual body and energetic brain will gather information and knowledge, which in some instances will allow you to seemingly "know" something that is going to take place in the future.

3) Translating information into the physical realm.

Your energetic brain will take this information, and while utilizing your spiritual senses, translate this information into the physical realm through your physical senses. This can take place many different ways, "seeing" something through pictures (clairvoyance), or "hearing" something or someone audibly (clairaudience), are some of the more common ways.

4) These pictures or gathered information will be accompanied by a noticeable "feeling" in the physical body.

This "feeling" will solidify that information was received and retained through your spiritual body. You will have a feeling in the chest or stomach area. Sometimes it will be felt throughout the entire body.

This "feeling" is one that is hard to describe:

Have you ever had a thought or feeling that you should or shouldn't do something?

Do you ever wonder if it's your mind or your intuition?

Many times people completely ignore their own intuition because they think it's something they are making up in their head, even when it's accompanied by a noticeable feeling in the body. So here is an easy way to help you to determine if they are intuitive "feelings" or not:

Intuitive feelings (What intuitive "feelings" feel like):

1) "I can't quite put my finger on it," or "I can't really describe it."
2) "I don't know."
3) "It just feels (or doesn't feel) right."
4) "It's hard to describe."
5) "I just know that I should (or shouldn't) do XYZ."

In other words, intuitive feelings are hard to describe or put an adjective to. When you have feelings that you cannot describe easily, that's usually an intuitive red flag or a sign that you're tapping into your intuition or psychic senses.

Non-intuitive feelings (What your "feelings" feel like):

1) Anxious
2) Sad
3) Happy
4) Depressed
5) Excited

Your own thoughts and non-intuitive feelings can usually be described very easily, because these types of feelings are usually more attached to wants, desires of an expected outcome, and control. If you can describe your feelings easily, it would take some more determination to see if you were tapping into your own intuition and psychic senses.

There is more to fully understanding this process. It takes place at the "meeting center" of the spiritual body and physical body, where there are energy centers or vortexes. These energy centers are commonly referred to as your chakras. Your chakras are another intricate part of your spiritual body which is often overlooked. Yet when learning about your spiritual body, intuition, and your psychic senses, it's extremely important for you to understand what role they play. Which brings us to our next chapter.

Your Spiritual Body & Chakras

Understanding chakras and your chakra system is important to having a better grasp on how the psychic process works. Your spiritual body and chakras are subjects I feel are overlooked when talking about intuition and psychic ability. Many teachers either don't have enough information themselves or just assume you already know this information, so I would like to cover some basic information here.

What is your chakra system? When you're born, your spiritual body enters and connects itself to your physical body through energy centers or vortexes. These energy centers are what are referred to as your Chakras or Chakra System. They're energy centers where your physical body and your spiritual body connect and meet. You have seven main chakras on the body and they each do different things. See the diagram on the following page.

The Seven Chakras

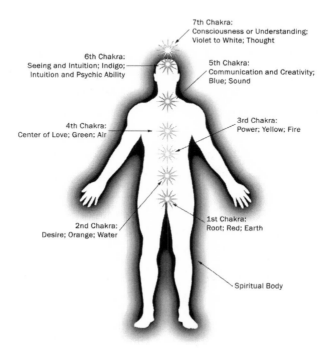

7th Chakra:
Consciousness or Understanding;
Violet to White; Thought

6th Chakra:
Seeing and Intuition; Indigo;
Intuition and Psychic Ability

5th Chakra:
Communication and Creativity;
Blue; Sound

4th Chakra:
Center of Love; Green; Air

3rd Chakra:
Power; Yellow; Fire

2nd Chakra:
Desire; Orange; Water

1st Chakra:
Root; Red; Earth

Spiritual Body

Even I didn't realize, until I started teaching psychic ability classes, that most people don't know where their chakras centers are on their own body. As you can see from the diagram, the chakra system lies right down the center of the body (equal distance from side to side), which is correct; however, the chakra centers themselves do not lie in the center of your entire body (or equal distance from front to back).

Your chakras are near your spine.

Most people see the diagrams and/or have read things that say they're down the center of the body, and assume this also means of equal distance between the front and back of your body. Many people believe the chakra system starts at the center of the top of your head and extends down through the center of the body. This isn't where the meeting point is (where your physical and spiritual bodies meet). The chakras do extend out to the center of your body and even beyond, but the meeting point is located near your spinal column.

So when you think of your chakras, imagine them starting near the crown of your head continuing down the center of your body (equal distance from side to side) and running along your spine to your tailbone area.

Why is this important? Because you will utilize the chakra system when utilizing your intuition and psychic senses, or even during spirit communication, when tapping into your spiritual body. In fact, chakras are a very important component in the process. Primarily, you will be working with chakras four, five, and six, and their meeting point is something with which you will become very familiar with during this process. It is also very important when learning how to develop your sensitivity level and learning more control as you advance. Since this isn't a book about the chakra system, I am only going to briefly touch upon them, in order to give you the information you need.

Three Important Things You Need To Know About Chakras

1) Chakra is "Sanskrit" for wheel or disk. They are spinning wheels of energy, or "vortexes." They filter energy from the environment and allow only matching vibrations in and rid the rest.

2) It's where psychic energy travels from the spirit realm to you in the physical realm (super important to know).

3) There are seven main chakra centers and they are each responsible for different things in your spiritual and physical bodies. Each of them are represented by a color.

I want to repeat something which is super important:

It's where psychic energy travels from the spirit realm to you in the physical realm.

If you don't have an understanding of this very important information, you won't be able advance your intuition and psychic senses to the best of your ability. Why? Because your physical body will begin to experience many feelings, as you begin to advance. These feelings will happen during the time you're receiving and translating information from your spiritual body at these chakra centers. It will help you begin to differentiate between valid information from your spiritual body and your own thoughts. It will validate what's happening with your spiritual body at the time. It will help you develop your abilities to the most advanced levels.

And most importantly, it will help to allow your mind to make sense of it all on a physical level.

Let's face it, it helps since we live in a physical world. When you allow your mind to become part of the process by allowing it to "make sense" of what is happening, your mind will aid you in learning how to develop this gift to the best of your ability. It will allow you to break through old belief systems by replacing them with new knowledge. If you don't replace old beliefs like, "how is this possible" with new knowledge of "it's possible and here is why. . .," your mind will fight to "make sense" of it all— it will become a hindrance and cause blockages.

More basic information on chakras:

1st Chakra
Root Chakra
(Color: Red)

- Earth chakra, it's your foundation
- Glands: adrenals

- Other Body Parts: legs, feet, bones, large intestine, teeth
- Malfunction: weight problems, hemorrhoids, constipation, sciatica, degenerative arthritis, knee troubles
- Purpose: to ground you like a lightning rod (very important in spiritual work), plugs your energy into the earth's energy. Grounding is a coping mechanism for stress.
- Survival chakra

2nd Chakra
Desire Chakra
(Color: Orange)

- Water chakra
- Glands: ovaries, testicles
- Body Parts: womb, genitals, kidney, bladder, circulatory system
- Malfunction: impotence, frigidity, uterine, bladder, or kidney trouble, stiff lower back
- Purpose: to let go and flow (movement). The center of sexuality, emotions, desire, sensation, pleasure, movement and nurturance. Related to the moon and its pull on energy.
- Clairsentience/empath is the psychic sense of the second chakra

3rd Chakra
Power Chakra
(Color: Yellow)

- Fire chakra
- Glands: pancreas, adrenals
- Body Parts: digestive system, muscles
- Malfunction: ulcers, diabetes, hypoglycemia, digestive disorders
- Purpose: transformation and personal power
- Intuition sits in this chakra—gut feeling

4th Chakra
The Center of Love
(Color: Green)

- Air chakra
- Glands: thymus
- Body Parts: lungs, heart, pericardium, arms, hands
- Malfunctions: asthma, high blood pressure, heart disease, lung disease
- Purpose: compassion and love
- Higher consciousness elevates and expands the heart chakra; therefore, it is sometimes utilized during spirit communication. Empaths also utilize this chakra.

5th Chakra
Communication/Creativity Chakra
(Color: Blue)

- Sound chakra
- Glands: thyroid, parathyroid
- Body Parts: neck, shoulders, arms, hands
- Malfunction: sore throat, stiff neck, colds, thyroid problems, hearing problems
- Purpose: communication and creativity, communication through sound, vibration, self-expression, and creativity. It includes listening, speaking, writing, telepathy and any of the arts. As your creative chakra, artists and musicians utilize this chakra consistently.
- Channeling information from the spirit realm, channels utilize this chakra almost always during spirit communication.

6th Chakra
Seeing and Intuition
(Color: Indigo)

- Intuition and psychic ability chakra
- Glands: pineal
- Body Parts: eyes
- Malfunction: blindness, headaches, nightmares, eye-strain, blurred vision
- Purpose: development of psychic abilities
- Clairvoyance or clear seeing

7th Chakra
Consciousness or Understanding Chakra
(Color: Violet to White)

- Thought chakra
- Gland: pituitary
- Body Parts: cerebral cortex, central nervous system
- Malfunctions: depression, alienation, confusion, boredom, apathy, inability to learn
- Purpose: this chakra is the seat of enlightenment
- The function is thought and knowing or claircognizance

Now that you know the basics, it's important you pay particular attention to chakras four, five, and six. Chakra four is between the shoulder blades; chakra five is located at the back of your neck, and chakra six is located at back of your head (directly on the opposite side of where your eyes are). Why these three? Because chakras will activate when you are working with developing your intuition, psychic ability or spirit communication. Those chakras open and they open wide!

When I first started to develop my own psychic ability and spirit communication to an advanced level, this was something which really confused me. I'd be walking around, constantly feeling like there was a huge gaping hole in the back of my neck, and sometimes I could feel a hole in between my shoulder blades as well. I could tell they were clearly two different holes; they didn't run into each other, they felt very separate to me. Sometimes these holes felt so big it seemed as if someone could put a fist in there. The weird thing was I knew there was no hole, so what was going on?

I asked almost everyone about it who I thought would know. Nobody knew what it was. These were all very advanced psychics, some of the best I've ever seen. Even one of the greatest channelers in the country, who I happened to know at the time, didn't know what to tell me. Don't get me wrong, they all knew what "feeling" I was talking about. They'd say things like, "Of course, that's just what happens when you begin to develop psychically." They all even experienced the same thing. But it wasn't until many years later when my own counsel, who I channel, told me what it was. It was my chakra centers, opening and closing.

This is when I discovered most teachers (many who are very advanced themselves) don't teach about this particular experience because they either don't quite understand it themselves, they are experiencing it, sure, but they don't realize it's their chakras, or they just assume and take it for granted that you know what this big, gaping hole is. When I made this connection, it allowed me to take my psychic ability and spirit communication to a whole new level. It allowed me to have a lot more control over how and what was happening. It allowed me to finally feel like I had gained access to some type of psychic control panel!

This open feeling you will experience is your chakra or chakra centers. It's the "meeting point" or the place in which your two bodies meet. It allows information to be received from the spiritual realm. The information is then transferred to your physical body through this "meeting point" to your physical senses.

As you become aware of them, you can learn to open and close these centers at will, but when you're first developing, you may walk around feeling "open" in the back. They will usually activate at random, and it can be really annoying when you're at the movie theater! You may feel them open all at once, or it could be one at a time, it makes no difference. The way in which they open, and which ones open at what time, is unique to each individual.

To sum up the last couple of chapters: Your spiritual body is an energetic body, which is made up of your Soul DNA (spiritual genetic system) and the essence of who you are, spiritual senses (psychic senses), energy centers and vortexes (chakras and chakra system), as well as an energetic brain that directs and harmonizes everything. It has many functions, some of which have been listed here, however, we've just barely scratched the surface of others.

Your spiritual body serves a distinct purpose in the physical world; it gives your physical body "life."

You wouldn't be here learning to develop your intuition and psychic ability in this world otherwise.

Your "Spiritual GPS"

In order to utilize intuition and psychic ability properly, there is one very important thing which you must know ... *your psychic senses serve a very specific purpose.* Many people do not know this. They don't know there is a reason you are gifted with intuition and psychic ability; it's not just for fun. Just like your physical senses such as your eyesight, touch, smell, hearing and taste all serve a purpose. Your psychic senses do the same thing, only in a different way. Before we get into that a bit further, it's important that you know the following three things.

Three Important Things Your Should Know About Intuition & Psychic Ability:

1) Each and every one of us is born *with intuition and psychic ability.*

2) Intuition and psychic ability is meant to be used on a *daily basis.*

3) *Intuition and psychic ability has a very specific purpose: "It is your spiritual GPS."*

So what is your Spiritual GPS?

"Spiritual GPS" is your spiritual guidance system. A guidance system, which is built into your Soul DNA, with a specific purpose, to help guide you towards the best possible outcome for you. Always ...

Intuition and psychic ability has a clearly defined purpose! Most of the time, it is viewed as entertainment, something to do for fun, or something interesting to play around with. However, its purpose is rather important. Everyone should know what this purpose is, it should not be taken lightly, and it should not be easily dismissed.

Intuition and psychic ability is meant to help you bring into your life everything which you desire. It is meant to help you live the most amazing life possible.

It is meant to make life easier ...

So why is it not helping to "make life easier" for some people? For many different reasons:

1) Because people do not understand psychic ability and what it is used for, since they have trouble validating it in the physical realm, it has been under scrutiny for years.

2) It is a guidance system, and guidance can easily be ignored.

3) People tend to trust other people's opinions, more than they trust themselves.

4) People have learned to follow other people's successes and failures, instead of finding their own way and their own path. (Intuition and psychic ability works with your own journey, it is not effective if you are trying to follow someone else's blueprint).

5) *Most people have no idea it has a specific purpose!*

Numbers one and two are easy and pretty self-explanatory. But let's talk about number three for a minute. You are built with your own internal guidance system. A guidance system which knows your very own wants and needs better than anyone else on the planet. Yet many people push aside their own intuition for someone else's opinion on what they should do in a given situation. Or what they should do in life! Now granted, it is helpful to weigh in other people's opinions and draw knowledge from their own life experiences every once in a while. But to do this on a daily or weekly basis makes absolutely no sense!

Here is what I mean. Imagine you are traveling to a new town. A town which you have never been to before, in search of a specific destination. However, you have a pretty good idea of where this destination is. When you arrived in this new town, you rent a car, put all of your things into your vehicle and off you go. This vehicle is quite nice; it is new and up to date, equipped with its very own working GPS system. But you decide not to turn it on; "Who needs that?" you think to yourself. "Any smart person can surely find their way around." With that thought in mind, you decide you can find your destination on your own. You drive for several miles, but after awhile, you realize you seem to be going in circles. You feel as if you're not getting any closer to where you want to be. You're beginning to get confused. None of the roads look familiar to you since you have never been here before. Then, you come up upon some crossroads, it's official ... you're lost! You don't know which way to go or what road to take. You stop and look around for a minute, trying to decide what to do next, but instead of turning on your own perfectly working GPS system in your car, and allowing it to help guide you towards your destination, you grab your cell phone, quickly dial a friend, who happens to be in another state, and say, "Hey, I'm lost. Can you go out to your car, turn on your GPS and tell me what it says I should do?"

What sense would that make to have someone who is not in the same place you are at the moment use his or her guidance system (from where they are) to help you navigate your way to your destination? Especially when you have a perfectly reliable guidance system of your own the whole time? Yet people do it all of the time! They want to know what their friends and family think they should do regarding love, money, and career. They ask for their advice and opinions on everything. For some reason people think other people have a more reliable guidance system than they have themselves. But it really all comes down to trust.

You need to learn to trust your own instincts or psychic senses ....

Like I mentioned before, it's okay to occasionally ask someone for his or her opinion, and use it to weigh in on your own decision-making. But this rarely happens. What does happen, however, is people will disregard their own "intuitive feelings" if another person can make a "valid argument" to why they should or shouldn't do something. If this argument or point seems rational, people will go against their own guidance system and make different choices. Choices based on someone else's guidance system.

There are several problems with making decisions based on someone else's guidance system:

1) Many times people will tell you what they think you should do based on *what they want you to do.*

Now you might be thinking, "No, everyone I know has my best interest at heart!" While that could be true, those same people base their opinions on their own fears, worries and what they feel comfortable with at the time. Do you want to live your life and make your decisions based on someone else's fears, worries, and comfort level? Just think about it. How many times in your life have you wanted to do something that terrifies someone else, like moving, skydiving, or switching jobs? And how many times did your friends and family support you, and tell you to go for it, despite having their own fears and worries, because they knew it was your desire to do so? Probably not many. I'm not talking about jumping into a container full of spiders, or searching for the deadliest snake in the world, or even something like skydiving. I'm talking about things such as moving states, choosing a non-traditional career, getting married or divorced, buying a house or a car, or traveling abroad, these things terrify the daylights out of people! Most people think you must go to college and get a college degree in order to make a good living, so if you choose not to, you will be poor! Not true. Many people are also terrified of uprooting themselves and moving. So they will have strong opinions like, "How are you going to find a job? The cost of living is so much higher there! What about your friends and family?" I know, because I heard all of those things when I moved to Hawaii. And good luck if you wish to travel the world! Your friends and family will almost be certain that it will cause you to go into massive debt, on the verge of bankruptcy, it will be so expensive. (Not true, since the U.S is one of the most expensive places in the world to live). If you make it past bankruptcy, you will probably be robbed at gunpoint (Since the only safe place to travel is the U.S.? Um ... ya ... I have heard this one, too!) Or you will be kidnapped and held for ransom. (In which case they will not pay the ransom, because they told you not to go in the first place, and you should learn your lesson!) Then you will return penniless, with no job to return to (since you were gone way too long from the whole kidnapping incident), to a miserable life. I'm sure you get the point.

People will guide you based on their own fears and worries at the time; they can't help it, it's human nature.

2) People have very different views of happiness and success.

One of the most sought after things in life is happiness. But how everyone defines happiness, is very different. What might make one person extremely happy, may have the opposite affect on someone else. Since we are all very individual people, trying to guide someone else towards their own happiness (unless you are trained to do so), can be next to impossible. Why? Because finding happiness is an individual journey. You are the only one who can find happiness within. You are the only one who truly knows what makes you happy. Your guidance system is wired to help guide you in the proper direction of your own happiness. You see, other people's guidance system is wired to help guide them towards their own happiness. This is why many times, without even realizing it, people will guide you towards their own happiness. They can't help it, they are wired that way.

Intuition and psychic ability serves a very specific purpose, to help guide you towards the best possible direction for you. Everyone is trying to figure life out to the best of their ability, but they are not always right, so don't rely on them for your answers, then turn around and blame them when they are wrong. Your friends and family should be supporters; they are not here to hold your hand in attempts to help guide your spiritual self through this physical world. They are in the same boat as you, they're trying to figure out their own journey. They have different perspectives, they have lived different lives and they are on different journeys of their own.

You may not understand your spiritual guidance system, but it's important that you learn to trust it. Trust that it has a purpose. Trust that it is given to you to help your spiritual self navigate though this physical world. Trust that it is given to you to help make life easier …

What Are Your
Psychic Senses?

Much like your physical senses, your spiritual or psychic senses were given to you with a specific purpose in mind. Your psychic senses are a faculty by which external or outside stimuli (information or knowledge), are received and felt. Even though psychic ability is one of your spiritual senses, your spiritual body works very closely in conjunction with the physical body and your physical senses, such as touch, taste, hearing, seeing and smelling. In fact, your spiritual body relies on your physical senses to help in its translation of the information that has been received. In other words, even though you are gaining information through your spiritual body, this information must be translated into the physical world in order for it to be useful to us.

There are many different ways in which this happens. Here are some of the more common psychic senses in no particular order:

Clairvoyance
Clairsentience/Empath
Clairaudience
Claircognizance
Clairtangency
Clairgustance
Clairscent

When you are developing your psychic senses, most likely you will not develop or utilize all of these abilities. In fact, it is rare that someone will have developed each and every one of these senses. What usually happens is you will become stronger in some areas, utilizing two or three of them primarily. It is then possible for you to experience some of the other gifts listed here at different times in your life. So don't be disappointed and think something is wrong, or worry that you're not developing your psychic ability properly if you have not experienced all of these things. Sometimes you may only experience one of these things, and that's perfectly fine. Every individual is different, so everyone's gifts are different. They are developed to different degrees or used in different combinations. On the same note, if you ever have a psychic reading, do not assume that all psychics are the same. Each and every one of them can see things in their own unique way. So understand that not all psychics are clairvoyant or clairaudient. They might not have either of those gifts. It is perfectly fine to ask them if you are wondering what gifts they do have and what gifts they utilize during a psychic reading.

I'm going to talk about each one of these psychic senses on a more individual level so you have a better understanding of each of them. But first I'm going to give you a couple of exercises which will help you get in touch with your psychic senses and help you develop them.

Psychic Senses Exercise #1

In preparation for this exercise you will need another person's help. In fact, it would be a good idea for you to partner with someone for these exercises since the next exercise is a partner exercise.

Preparation:

1) You will need five containers. Any type of container, boxes or bags that you cannot see through will do. It's good to try and keep them somewhat similar in size.

2) You will need five objects. Get your helper to go around the house and find five different objects, which will fit into each of the containers.

3) Have the containers placed in front of you. After your helper finds five objects, have them place the objects into the containers, and place the containers in front of you in a straight line from right to left, so that you can see all of the containers lined up at the same time.

4) You will need a pen and a piece of paper. Place the pen and paper near your chair so they can be easily grabbed.

Meditation: It is helpful if your helper can read this part to you slowly. However, if you choose to do it by yourself, just read through the meditation first, then do the meditation.

1) Sit comfortably in a chair or in an upright position in a quiet place.

2) Close your eyes and concentrate on your breathing. Slow your breathing to a relaxed state.

3) When your breathing is rhythmic, concentrate on relaxing all of the muscles in your body.

4) Ask yourself, "If my intuitive mind had a color, what would it be?" Take a minute to see what color appears to you. It may be appear to be solid or it may change colors.

5) Next, ask yourself, "If my intuitive mind had a symbol, what would it be?" Take a minute to see what appears. It could be an object, an animal, or a written symbol. Relax and feel the symbol.

6) Then ask yourself, "If my intuitive mind had a sound, what would it be?" Take a minute and

listen. You will most likely hear a sound as if you are recalling a noise you have heard in the past. This is called hearing with your inner ear. Or you may just see an object, which represents a sound. Spend a minute or two familiarizing yourself with the sound.

7) Ask yourself, "If my intuitive mind had a smell, what would it be?" Take a minute to see what you smell. You may be able to detect a scent in the air. Or an object might appear to you, representing a scent or smell, which is fine, too.

8) Next, ask yourself, "If my intuitive mind had a taste, what would it be?" You may get a faint taste of something or you may see an object that represents a certain flavor to you. Relax and feel the flavor.

9) Lastly, ask yourself, "If my intuitive mind had a food it wanted you to eat, what would it be?" Take a minute to see what appears. It might be one food or a combination of foods. Take your time and observe what appears. If you do not know what it is, observe its size, color and shape.

10) You may open your eyes and grab your pen and paper.

11) Now, look at the first container. Using all of the psychic senses that you just experimented with, I want you to observe your sense of smell, hearing, taste, and your mind's eye. Ask yourself, "What do I feel when I look at the container?" Write down anything that comes to mind … don't think about it, or analyze what you are experiencing, just write. Ask yourself, "What color do I feel?" and write down what comes to mind. Allow anything into your thoughts, if you see a sun, a horse, the color orange, a number, anything that you are feeling is valid. There is no right or wrong here.

12) Take your time and do this with each individual container. Do not rush this, it may take a couple of minutes or it may take five minutes, but keep yourself feeling unhurried and relaxed during this exercise.

13) After you have gone down and written something about each container, open each one, one at a time, and see what's inside.

14) *Don't try and see how you were wrong, see how you can make the connection!* In other words, if you wrote down yellow, and it's a pair of dark sunglasses, yellow makes sense as it represents the sun. If you wrote down something relating to the outdoors and the object was a sneaker, it makes sense also because you put on sneakers to go outside.

When you try and see how you can "make the connection" it will help you to train and strengthen your psychic senses, and hone this skill.

You will almost always be able to make some kind of connection. Connection equals strength when developing your abilities. With each "connection" your psychic senses gain strength and they will begin to look for the connection on their own each time you try and utilize them in the future. It is just like when you are teaching a child something or training an animal. You are teaching and "training" your psychic senses what to look for, you are training your senses to seek out the "connection."

When you are learning to utilize your psychic senses again, you must retrain them to seek out what you're looking for. The more you do this exercise and see where the connection is, the better and better you will become. You will most likely surprise yourself.

Psychic Senses Partner Exercise #2

This is an exercise in which you and a partner will work together, taking turns. First make sure that each of you go through the meditation part as before:

Meditation: (You can skip this part if you just did it during exercise #1).

1) Sit comfortably in a chair or in an upright position in a quiet place.

2) Close your eyes and concentrate on your breathing. Slow your breathing to a relaxed state.

3) When your breathing is rhythmic, concentrate on relaxing all of the muscles in your body.

4) Ask yourself, "If my intuitive mind had a color, what would it be?" Take a minute to see what color appears to you, it may be solid or it may change colors.

5) Next, ask yourself, "If my intuitive mind had a symbol, what would it be?" Take a minute to see what appears. It could be an object, an animal, or a written symbol.

6) Then, ask yourself, "If my intuitive mind had a sound, what would it be?" Take a minute and listen. You will most likely hear a sound as if you are recalling a noise you have heard in the past. This is called hearing with your inner ear.

7) Ask yourself, "If my intuitive mind had a smell, what would it be?" Take a minute to see what you smell. An object might appear to you, representing a scent or smell, which is fine, too.

8) Next ask yourself, "If my intuitive mind had a taste, what would it be?" You may get a faint taste of something or you may see an object that represents a certain flavor to you.

9) Lastly, ask yourself, "If my intuitive mind had a food it wanted you to eat, what would it be?" Take a minute to see what appears.

10) Open your eyes.

Intuitive Reading: Sit directly across from one another. One person will be the reader and the other one will give the information. Then you will switch.

1) Give the name and age of someone your partner does not know: The person giving the information should tell the reader the name and age of a person who they are thinking of. The reader should then close their eyes for a minute and say anything they sense or "feel" with their five senses. It might be a description such as height, weight, or hair color, or it might be emotions such as being happy, sad, or depressed. There could be a smell such as oil, brownies, or flowers. Or you may see a location; just say whatever you are sensing.

Remember there is no right or wrong answer, many times, if the information is not matching the person they mentioned, you are most likely picking up on another person.

2) The information giver can then verify what is correct: It's helpful if the person giving the information nods or acknowledges when the reader is "hitting" on something. It helps the reader to follow that feeling, instead of searching for others. You can go as long as you wish. Then switch and give the other person and name and age of someone you know.

Past Life Reading: One person will ask their partner some questions to help them recall a past life. Then you will switch.

1) Have your partner close their eyes (assuming you have already done the meditation from above). Ask them to relax a minute and get comfortable. After they clear their mind, when they are ready, ask them, "If you were in another life would you be male or female?" Give them time to answer, do not rush them, however, if they are stuck, you can move to the next one.

2) Next, ask them, "In this other life, how old would you be?" Have them tell you the first thing that pops into their head. *Encourage them to relax and "feel" for the answer.*

3) Continue with these questions, each one followed by proper time to answer. (This should be very relaxing and not rushed):

"Where would you live?"

"What do your surroundings look like?"

"What do your clothes look like?"

"Do you know what year it is?"

"Are you married?"

"Do you work?"

"What do you do during the daytime?"

"Do you have a family?"

4) Allow the flow to continue until you feel it is done. It's very common for the person who is asking the questions to "see" the other person's lifetime or have a very good "sense" of who they were, also.

5) Then switch places, and do it again.

Object Reading: One person will give their partner a personal object for them to read, then you will switch.

1) Give the reader a personal item. This can be something like jewelry, a journal, cell phone, keys, a credit card, or a trinket. It is good to use something meaningful, if possible.

2) Hold the object and close your eyes. Take a minute to relax and clear your mind. Then concentrate on the object you are holding.

3) "Feel" what comes to mind. You will begin to see

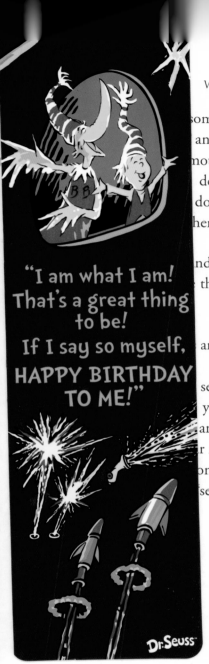

"I am what I am!
That's a great thing
to be!
If I say so myself,
**HAPPY BIRTHDAY
TO ME!**"

Dr.Seuss

WHAT ARE YOUR PSYCHIC SENSES?

something about the object. Tell anything that comes to mind, motion, a smell, a picture, or a detail you pick up, say it out don't be afraid to be wrong, as here.

nd see if the other person can the connection" to what it was

and do it again.

senses, it is all about "feeling" your eyes and "feel" from the answer from there. When your mind out of the equation and on what you are feeling without see" psychically.

Clairvoyance (Clear Seeing)

First we are going to talk about clairvoyance, especially since this is the most talked about of the psychic senses. What is clairvoyance?

Clairvoyance is French, with clair meaning "clear" and voyance meaning "vision." It refers to the ability to gain information about an object, person, location, or physical event through means of seeing pictures.

There are two ways in which you can be clairvoyant. Some people can see things visually, in the same manner as you see all of your surroundings right now. Or you can have visions or see pictures in what is called your mind's eye. Seeing things in your mind's eye is far more common and something that can be easily developed with training and practice. Since this is far more common, we will talk about how this works first.

Seeing Clairvoyantly Through Your "Mind's Eye"

Your mind's eye is referred to as your visual memory or imagination. It is commonly associated with the 6th chakra in the center of your forehead.

When using clairvoyance, although you are using what is referred to as your "visual memory," you are not recalling a memory from the past, although the process can feel very similar to recalling a memory. In fact, that's often how I describe what happens when I see the future to people. It feels like when you remember something that happened yesterday, only you're looking into the future because it hasn't happened yet, so it kind of feels like you're remembering the future. Weird, right? The reason it feels more like a memory is because when you recall a memory, you recall it as an actual event that has taken place. *You can feel it in your whole body as fact.*

If you want to further understand what it feels like, and what I'm talking about, you can try this:

1) Recall A Memory: Sit comfortably in a chair, close your eyes, and relax. Think back to an event that happened yesterday, or this week. Think of an event that most stands out to you and your memory. Recall what happened during that time, recall the events that took place surrounding that memory. Recall who was there and what might have been said. When you recall this memory, pay attention to

how it feels in the body. How does it feel in the chest area? It's a solid feeling, a factual feeling, as something that has already occurred. Your body will recognize it and you will feel it to the core of your being as fact.

Next.

2) Use Your Imagination: Sit in a chair and close your eyes. Imagine something you would like to see happen in the future. It might be going on a trip, buying a house, seeing a movie, having a better relationship with someone in your life. It can be big or small, it's up to you. Now imagine how this event could take place, and what might actually happen in the future regarding this particular scenario. Pay attention to how your body feels regarding this future event. How do you feel in the chest area or overall body? Most likely it does not have the solid "knowing" or "factual feeling" that your memory did. It will not feel as solid, more like it is a possibility or that it is probable, and that feeling will be sprinkled with a bit of uncertainty. That is the difference.

When you develop a gift of clairvoyance, you will have a vision or what feels like "a memory" of a future event that is going to take place, which is accompanied by a strong "factual" feeling in the body.

It feels as if this event has already happened, even though it hasn't. Now most good clairvoyants can also "sense" or even "see" future events leading up to this vision if they wish to. So don't worry if you see something you don't wish to take place. We'll get into this more a bit later.

Here are some exercises, which will help you to understand what it feels like to see with your mind's eye:

#1 Observe the Alpha State

As you fall asleep at night, notice your relaxed mental state. When you find your mind wandering wildly and you begin to see dreamlike images in your mind's eye, you are in what is referred to as the Alpha state. Pay attention to what this Alpha state feels like whenever you go to sleep, and learn to recognize this state when you are meditating or during times of relaxation. Really observe the dreamlike images by allowing them in, don't force anything, observe the state of allowing, the state of no resistance. This is the key; relax and allow, relax and allow.

These Alpha experiences are very similar to what many mediums experience when communicating with spirits. When you do this exercise you will become familiar with the state you will experience when using clairvoyance. During this time, you naturally let your guard down as you are preparing yourself to be spiritually aligned, through sleep. As part of the process, you allow pictures to come in with no resistance. This is an ability everyone has; it's just that not many people realize how useful it is. By doing this exercise you'll become consciously aware of what it's like to receive and recognize the faint mental impressions that occur during spirit communication. You'll become very aware of the state of allowing, with no attachments to what is coming in and what is going out. You should do this every night until you begin to feel the resistance of psychically "seeing" things diminish during your waking hours.

#2 Visualizing In the "Mind's Eye"

You see through your mind's eye all of the time, like you have just learned. You probably called it remembering or imagining. Remembering or imagining uses the same process of seeing with your "mind's eye."

What it is you are "seeing" is what separates a memory from seeing something clairvoyantly.

When you "remember" in your mind's eye, you were there, so you remember it. When you "see" something clairvoyantly, through telepathy or your "mind's eye," you see it as if you remember it, only you never had that particular experience to remember. So it is new information you see through the "mind's eye."

1) You will need a box of crayons, or you can use something similar, like colored markers or pencils.

2) Sit on the floor or at the table, then dump them out in front of you and mix them all up.

3) Center yourself. Close your eyes and quiet your mind. Preferably do the short meditation exercise that you learned before to get your psychic senses heightened.

4) Draw a color. With your eyes closed, draw a color. Then "feel" for the color. Ask yourself, "What does this color feel like?" A color or a shade will pop into your head, or an object representing that color. When this happens, open your eyes and see what it is!

Now don't get discouraged if you're wrong, as this exercise is meant to do a number of times, resulting in an overall average of success. To help put things in perspective for you, here are some averages:

Correct 17% of the time is considered average for people not utilizing psychic senses.

Correct 33% of the time is considered average for most psychics.

Correct 34% + of the time, above average of most psychics.

The purpose of this exercise is to help you become familiar with how it "feels" to see things in the mind's eye. These exercises are also designed to be a part of the training process for your spiri-

tual body. The same way you exercise and train your physical body for something physical, you must also exercise and train your spiritual body in order to help you perform spiritual tasks as well.

Seeing Clairvoyantly Without Your "Mind's Eye"

If you have the gift and ability to see clairvoyantly without your mind's eye, you'll already know it; in other words, it won't be news to you. But for those of you who don't, I would like to explain what it's like a bit more.

Mediums primarily have this gift, not all, but some of them have this ability. This gift is primarily utilized when seeing spirits, Spirit Guides, Angels, and ghosts. Imprints of old structures can also sometimes be seen. Many times when you see spirits in this manner, they will not appear to be completely solid energetically, but they will have a certain transparent quality about them, which helps you to determine the difference between the physical realm and the spiritual realm. This is not always the case, but it's the case more often than not.

It's not uncommon for children to have this ability. They don't think much of it until they get older, then as young adults, because of their newly formed belief system, it begins to freak them out. So they'll begin to tune it out as much as possible. It's a process most of us go through with many of our psychic gifts, unfortunately.

My son is clairvoyant, and often when he was very young, he would see his Spirit Guide. He would mention seeing "Frank" every now and again when he was around the house. Most nights he would tune in and visually see his guide. He would describe him to me as, "He looks the same as everyone else I see, only more see through." Much of the time his Spirit Guide would be walking on the front porch of our home, or he would show up at the end of his bed while he was sleeping. He would notice him if he woke up in the middle of the night. Now in most instances, this would startle the majority of kids. They would run to tell their parents, everyone would think the house was haunted, and they would all want to move! Luckily for him, I was well aware of what he was seeing, and spirits were nothing to be afraid of in our household. They were a part of our life, so it was "normal" to feel them or see them. Needless to say, those experiences were not nearly as scary as they could have been, had the environment been one that had taken on the perspective or belief of spirits being scary.

My son could see him clearly, and he would describe him in great detail. His guide was about six feet tall with dark hair and dark eyes. He dressed in a black suit, with a white undershirt, an overcoat, and a fedora hat. The era of dress was consistent with his Spirit Guide's last lifetime here on earth. We know this because when my son was older, I did a past life regression on him (my kids used to love to do this for fun), and he had a very clear memory of being with his Spirit Guide during one of his last lifetimes, sometime in the very early 1900s. He could see they worked together in that lifetime and he knew roughly where they lived. He knew his friend saved his life and that they were very good friends throughout that existence.

Dressing in the era of their last existence together may have been an attempt to try and present himself in a manner that my son would recognize him, or potentially trigger some internal memory, as not to frighten him. Or maybe he just liked the suit.

So clearly you can see the difference here; one gift you can develop very easily and one gift you are primarily "born" with.

Clairsentience (Feeling) or Empath

Clairsentience is what is more commonly referred to as an empath. It refers to a form of extrasensory perception where a person acquires psychic knowledge primarily by means of emphatic feelings and emotions. In other words, you can "feel" what's going on with another person emotionally.

This can absolutely be one of the most confusing of the psychic senses.

It's very common for children to develop this ability and it can be one of the hardest to cope with, especially if you don't know what is happening. When you are an empath, when you feel other people's emotions, your mind and body become a bit confused. Your body feels, or experiences, exactly what other people are experiencing at that particular time, and not what your mind signals your body that it is experiencing. This leaves your mind and body with mixed signals, like they're not on the same page. It takes a few minutes to process, but your thoughts and perceptions trigger your emotions and your emotional response. Therefore, your mind and its thoughts trigger your physical body to have an emotional response, causing a reaction. When this does not happen, say your physical body and its emotions are reacting on their own, without being triggered, your mind then searches for the reason. You assume it is you, when it is not you at all.

Your body mirrors or mimics someone else's emotions!

In other words, your body is duplicating how someone else is feeling. It's most commonly experienced when another person is right in front of you. For instance, if someone has had a very bad day, upon meeting up with them, they may put on a very happy face, and disguise their true emotions which they're experiencing at the time. They may act as if everything is wonderful, but in their presence you can feel what they are truly experiencing in that moment. You feel upset or sad for no reason. (Your mind and body are not on the same page. Since you had a good day, it makes no sense.) When this person walks away, however, you feel like your normal self again. As an empath, your body will mimic another person's true emotions when you think of them, or you are in their presence.

Children often experience empathy. I remember when my children where young, upon meeting someone I would say, "What did you think of so and so?" and sometimes their answer and observation would not reflect what that person was trying to project. In fact, many times it would be very different. Parents often do not realize their own children are usually naturally very connected and empathetic to their parents' feelings. So if the parent is consistently angry or upset, even when trying to hide it, your children most likely can "feel" right through your cover.

Six Signs You Are An Empath

1) Do you feel "overwhelmed" when going to a place filled with a lot of people?

2) Can you always tell when someone is lying to you?

3) Do you have random emotions or mood swings, especially when in someone else's presence, or when you think about them, which makes no sense to you.

4) Can you feel someone else's physical ailments?

5) Do you instinctively know what someone needs to feel better emotionally or physically?

6) Do you feel emotionally of physically drained after being around an individual, or a group of people, to the point of needing to take a nap, or physically not feeling well?

Every Empath Should Learn This:

Bubble Yourself

This is just like it sounds. Before you go into a place filled with people, you need to bubble yourself. This is like a quick meditation but it doesn't have to take long. You can easily do this in a couple of minutes; it's just important that you do it. A quick two-minute bubble is way better than no bubble at all! In fact, that's all you really need. I'll walk you through the steps here.

1) Find a quiet place where you won't be disturbed. (However, if you forget to do this before you go out, you can do this in the car before you go in someplace easily enough).

2) Sit comfortably in an upright position, hands to your side and feet flat on the floor. Don't cross your hands, feet, or legs.

3) Close your eyes and concentrate on your breathing. Slow your breathing to a relaxed state.

4) When your breathing is rhythmic, concentrate on relaxing all of the muscles in your body.

5) Next, imagine a white light of pure, powerful energy coming down from above your head. This white light is from the Holy Spirit, God, or source (whatever you are comfortable with). Feel this energy come through the roof of your house or car, and allow it to gently enter your

system through your seventh chakra, or the top of your head. This energy feels good, empowering, and protective.

6) Allow this white light energy to touch each chakra while it recharges your spiritual body. Continue to let the white light flow through your system until you feel fully charged.

7) Next, allow the excess energy to fill a bubble around you. "Feel and direct" this white light energy by way of thought to form a large bubble surrounding around your entire being. This powerful white light is recharging your energetic field with new energy, strong and protective energy. Feel this energy charging your system as it continues out into the bubble. Once the bubble is full, feel the strength of the bubble. Nothing can penetrate the bubble from the outside. It is like a protective barrier around your being.

8) Remain in this state until you feel a sense of completion, then release this image into the Universe and go about your day.

There is no right or wrong as to the time you spend creating the bubble, you should adjust the time to whatever feels right to you. This bubble works as a barrier to outside energies. It will protect you against other people's energy (or energy vampires), who are trying to draw energy from you, unknowingly. It will also help to protect you from a flood of emotions coming at you all at once when around a large group of people. It's harder for you to pick up their "radio signal," as the bubble dissipates it. These things are what leave you feeling shaky, weird and light headed.

When you keep your spiritual and physical bodies in harmony, it will strengthen your system in a very powerful way. It will allow you to have more control over the energies flowing in and out of your body. Exercise also grounds your system, which releases excess energy to dissipate into the earth very quickly; it's much faster than if you're just sitting around. And as an empath you're picking up excess stuff every day, from everywhere.

If you'd like to learn more on empathic senses and how to deal with them, please refer to the companion volume, Energy Vampires.

Clairaudience (Hearing)

Next we are going to talk about clairaudience. What is clairaudience?

Clairaudience is French, with clair meaning "clear" and audience meaning "hearing." It refers to the ability to gain information about an object, person, location, or physical event through means of hearing.

Clairaudience is essentially the ability to hear in a paranormal manner. Although most people think of it as the ability to hear something audibly, it does not just refer to actual perception of sound, but may instead indicate impressions of the "inner mental ear," similar to the way many people think words without having auditory impressions.

Just like with clairvoyance, there are two ways in which you can be clairaudient. Some people can hear things audibly, in the same manner as you hear the noise in your surroundings right now, such as a dripping faucet, cars driving by, or someone talking to you. However, you can also hear things with your "inner ear," such as remembering a song you heard on the radio, or a conversation you had with someone yesterday. When you are clairaudient, hearing things with your "inner ear" is far more common than hearing with your "outer ear," and something which can be developed with training and practice.

Clairaudience is primarily used to receive "guidance" from spirit or source.

This guidance may be from someone such as a Spirit Guide, Angels, or other spirits who have passed over. Whether you're hearing things with your "inner ear" or your "outer ear," guidance is the primary purpose. Because of this, psychics and mediums often utilize this ability when connecting with Spirit Guides, Angels and spirits from the other side, as it is a very common form of spirit communication. Since hearing with the "inner ear" is far more common, we will talk about how this works first.

#1 Hearing With the "Inner Ear"

You may or may not have heard this term before: "inner ear." However, it is a term which you will become very familiar with when learning to develop your intuition and psychic ability, or when learning more about spirit communication. When you hear things in your head from the "inner ear," it sounds like it's coming from within your inner being, instead of outside of your being like when you hear with the outer ear.

For instance, you know how it *feels and sounds* when you recall a conversation you've had in the past, or you remember a song you've recently heard on the radio? This is what it feels like to hear something with your "inner ear," only it's not information which you are reaching for, or something you are trying to remember. When you're in a very relaxed state, it's information which is received and heard, from within. You may wonder, "How do I know it's not just my own thinking?" Because it's usually information that hasn't been reached for, it's just allowed or received. This process of hearing with the "inner ear" usually takes quite a bit of training and confirmation. It requires time and training, because in order for this type of communication to be effective, you need to develop a certain level of trust that you're receiving information from a source outside yourself, and not just making things up. Building that kind of trust takes some time, but it can be developed.

Like I mentioned before, this "inner ear" type of communication is primarily used and developed by people such as psychics and mediums; often they hear spirits with their inner ear even from a young age. Then, over time, they begin to develop this skill when they realize other people are not hearing what they are hearing.

#2 Hearing With the "Outer Ear"

Next, we have hearing with your "outer ear." This is just like it sounds, only worse! When you receive guidance from someone such as your Spirit Guides audibly, you can hear them just like you hear someone talking to you, only the tone of their voice is very different. You can clearly tell you're hearing it with your "outer ear," and it's not from this physical realm. The difference is it's usually louder, crisper and more startling. When tone or sound travels between dimensions, it comes through with a very unique sound, or pitch to it. It's very crisp to your eardrum and you immediately identify it as something you haven't heard before. This is your Spirit Guide's least favorite way to communicate with you for all of these reasons.

To give you an idea of what it's like, I'll tell you about the first audible experience I had with my Spirit Guide. Many years ago, when I was very young, I was in a large department store shopping by myself. During this time of my life, my family and I were in the midst of dealing with a very unstable family member. Needless to say, it was very difficult, and it was definitely taking a toll on everyone. While shopping, out of nowhere, I heard the most authoritative, powerful voice say, "Get out now!" The voice was so loud and crisp I was frozen in my tracks. I couldn't breathe, my heart began to race like someone was chasing me, but my legs felt like concrete, so I couldn't move. I looked over my shoulder because it sounded as if the voice had come from someone standing directly behind me. I was terrified to turn around, but as I did, I realized no one was there. So I looked around while scanning the store, and I looked at the door, but to my surprise, everyone seemed fine. There was no urgency at all! I immediately got my bearings after what felt like ten very long minutes (but in actuality was probably about twenty seconds), and after calming myself a bit, I realized from the tone of the voice that it wasn't a person, but my Spirit Guide. Still terrified, I looked around again to see what could be so dangerous that I had to get out now. Was there going to be a robbery? What was happening? When my eyes scanned the front door for the second time, I saw the troubled family member entering the store. This may not seem like a big deal to others, but at the time, the stress I was under was affecting my health, so I was very grateful to have avoided this encounter.

Now to be fair, I've also heard my son's Spirit Guide, Frank, audibly, just like I would hear a regular person talking to me. However, it was much less startling. His voice was softer and his tone was not so intense. With Frank, the matter was not so urgent, so his voice was not as powerful. And because there was no sense of urgency in his voice, the tone was not so loud.

During the encounter in the department store, my Spirit Guide was trying to contact me in an urgent way, so I would be more apt to listen, and not just blow it off, or not take the message seriously. After the department store experience, however, I did ask my Spirit Guides not to scare the daylights out of me like that again. So now when they wish to talk with me audibly, they whisper or speak lightly as not to shock my system. I much prefer it that way.

Hearing your Spirit Guide audibly is not very common, even for psychics and mediums. Most psychics and mediums receive information in some of the other forms that we've talked about, such as words, pictures, or "inner ear." So don't get discouraged if you haven't heard, or don't hear your Spirit Guides audibly; it's rare. In my opinion, you might even want to be happy about not hearing them that way!

Claircognizance (Knowing)

Claircognizance is a form of extrasensory perception where a person acquires psychic knowledge primarily by means of acquired knowledge. It's the ability to know something without a physical explanation why you know it, you just know.

It's one of the least talked about of the psychic senses, yet one of the most common ones to have.

This is one of the most interesting of the psychic senses to me, because it's so overlooked, yet so common. It's also tricky, because if you have it, you probably think everyone has it. So you may not know it's a psychic sense at all! You can have it and utilize this psychic sense "with or without" any of the other psychic senses. It's very common for claircognizance to pair up with the other senses, solidifying your psychic knowledge. But you could very well have had this gift your entire life, and not even know it! Until now…

Here is a story that tells you a little bit about my experience with claircognizance. Since I have had a strong psychic ability my whole life, I never grew up knowing what it's like to be what people call "normal." I grew up, naturally thinking that everyone was like me. It wasn't until I got older that I realized not everyone had the same abilities I did, and I was a little confused. Since birth, one of my many psychic abilities has been claircognizance—I would just "know" things. People would say, "How do you just know? You can't just know!" Well, you see, I thought everyone just knew things, so I thought it was weird they didn't "know" what I was talking about. I wondered why they weren't tapping into their own gifts and abilities. As I grew older, I realized I was indeed very different. People didn't understand what I was seeing, hearing, or what I was trying to explain. It became frustrating for me, so I just stopped talking to them about it.

When I was a teenager, I became really skeptical. This is a very natural occurrence. If you haven't tried to block your abilities before your teenage years, this is usually the time it happens. After much skepticism from friends and adults, I started to question my own abilities. I began to wonder, "How do I just know things? Other people don't just know things. How do I? What makes me different? How do I know I'm even right?" So I decided to pretend I was no longer psychic, easy as that! Well, it's not so easy. One morning while I was sitting in class, I had a very strong "feeling or knowing" that I should go home early. I thought, "Whatever. I'll just ignore it and it will go away." Until now, I usually followed my feelings because I thought they were a part of my guidance system. Since this had been the case up until that day, everything had always worked out fine. But this particular day, I decided to no longer "know" things. I was determined, so I shut out all of the thoughts for the rest of the day and ignored them. I'd done a really good job and had even forgotten about it by the time I was leaving school with a friend. I was about three blocks away when we got into a four-car accident. That was when I realized that ignoring "knowing" things didn't work for me. That was a huge lesson! Though my friend and I only had minor injuries, it was the last time I decided to "challenge" my own abilities.

Like I mentioned, claircognizance is tricky, especially if you have it on its own, without having yet developed the ability to hear or see things. Here are some questions that might help you to determine if you have this ability.

Four Signs of Claircognizance:

1) Have you always just "known" things, even when you where a child?

2) Have you always "known" if something is a good or a bad idea, yet if someone asks you how you know, you can't really explain why?

3) Do you "know" if you should or shouldn't do something, but it makes no sense to you how you know or why you know?

4) Do you experience a "knowing" of good or bad, do or don't, should or shouldn't, without having any details to back up this "knowing"? In other words, the "knowing" is strong, but the details are vague or absent as to why.

Just like being an empath, if you have the ability of being claircognizant, when you read this chapter, you will have an "aha" moment of, "That all makes sense now!" It's something which will resonate with you right away. In fact, these two sentences should sum it up for you very clearly.

This gift is the ability to "know" things in the absence of pictures or hearing things, without receiving any details of why.

Knowing to the very core of your being that something is fact, without being able to explain how you "know."

Clairtangency
(Clear Touching)

Clairtangency is the ability to handle an object or touch an area and perceive through your hands to obtain psychic knowledge about the article, its owner or history. It's also known as Psychometry.

It is the ability to feel energy from objects or spaces and receive a psychic impression of the people who have touched it, or been in and around it.

Now people mostly think of clairtangency as relating to only objects that you hold, but it can also relate to large objects such as a car, a building, or a monument. People often unknowingly possess this psychic sense as well, but it's not talked about enough for people to understand what it is.

People feel energy all of the time from everywhere; objects, other people, and places. They just tend to ignore what they're feeling. Instead of recognizing it's the energy of a person, place, or thing they don't like, they just decide it's the actual person, place, or thing they don't like. However, when and if the energy of those things shift, which happens all of the time, they will then experience a very different reaction.

Here's a list of things that will help you determine if you have experienced this psychic sense. And since clairtangency is so common, many of you will probably resonate with at least some of the things on this list right away.

Eight Signs of Clairtangency:

1) Do you have trouble buying used things you would wear from rummage sales or consignment stores such as clothing or jewelry because they "feel" weird to you, or you don't like they way they feel on?

Do you personally not hold any judgments of buying used clothing or jewelry items, yet when you try them on it feels "weird or uncomfortable" despite your wish to have it? Have you tried to buy used clothing items only to find they sit in your closet, or you end up selling them, or giving them away? Used items such as clothing or jewelry hold the energy of their owners. They also tend to hold emotional energy of what the owner might have experienced when wearing the object. So many times you'll pick up on this energy and you may not know what you're experiencing. New items tend not to have an energy attached to them, as other people have not worn them. When you wear an item, there is an energy transfer.

2) Do you have trouble buying used furniture or going into antique stores as the energy feels icky or strange, but you don't know why?

This is very similar to what happens with objects that you wear. Furniture or objects that might go into your home also will have energy attached to them from the various owners who handled the objects. However, there are a couple things that are a bit different. Usually furniture, furniture items, or antiques tend to have multiple people who have come into contact with them, even with one owner. Also, energy doesn't always attach in the same way to these types of items. Many times, you can clear the energy from the item a bit easier by cleaning or refinishing it.

3) Do you steer clear of pawnshops, as they really don't feel good to you?

Pawnshops tend to have a lot of negative or "icky" energy in the store and around the products inside. There is a very simple reason for this. Usually people who pawn items are looking for quick cash in desperation. That alone will leave a very unsettling energy in the store and on the objects there. If you can buy things from a pawnshop with ease, it's a pretty good indicator that you don't have this ability.

4) Do you ever find yourself wanting or not wanting to go into a restaurant or store, because of how the place feels to you?

Despite the outside appearance of a place, do you ever find yourself either being drawn into or being steered away without any reasonable explanation? This is because the energy of a place and the people who inhabit it will set the tone energetically. It can work either way; it might feel good or not so good depending on the energy that is constantly coming and going into the place.

5) Do you ever find that cluttered spaces make you feel uncomfortable?

Do cluttered spaces make you feel uncomfortable? This could be anything from a junk yard to going to someone's cluttered house, or even your own house when it's messy. Do you find you feel overwhelmed or anxious when surrounded by clutter? Clutter carries a lot of scattered energy, energy that parks itself in the space. This energy can be really intense when a lot of it is piled in one particular place.

6) Do you ever find that a messy house or workplace affects your mood and productivity?

Similar to cluttered spaces, a messy house or workplace will hold scattered energy. This energy, if not cleaned out of your space, can make it hard for you to focus and concentrate if you are clairtangent.

7) Do you ever feel the need to wash your hands after picking up or looking through used items?

Used items hold energy, so if you're sensitive to that, you may feel the need to wash your hands as it will "stick" to you when you touch them. A simple solution is to wash your hands with soap and water, as it will wash transferred energy away.

8) Do you ever feel the need to wash your hands after picking up rocks or crystals?

Rocks and crystals are some of the most powerful objects when it comes to "retaining and transferring" energy. So it's a no brainer what will frequently happen when you come into contact with them. They also produce their own energy, just like people, so there doesn't have to be any transfer of someone else's energy to you, as you may pick up their own energy. Their energy is powerful and you may not resonate with each and every one of them, so you may feel compelled to wash your hands when coming into contact with certain stones.

When you are clairtangent, you pick up a lot from the energy around you, so your space needs to feel energetically clean. Otherwise you can feel the cluttered energy around you and it feels uncomfortable. It leaves you with a muddy or murky feeling. Let's say that you were about to go swimming and you arrived at a very nice pool. The pool has nice, crystal clear water and you're excited to get in and cool off. You step into the pool, and although you cannot touch in some spots, you can see all the way to the bottom. So you relax and enjoy the pool while floating and swimming around. Then a landscaper comes with a wheelbarrow full of dirt to do some gardening. He needs to walk near the pool to get to his destination. Suddenly he slips and falls into the pool, wheel barrow and all! The water quickly becomes murky and dirty. You can no longer see the bottom and all you want to do is get out as soon as you can.

That's what it feels like when you're clairtangent. When you're in a space or you are around objects that feel "energetically clean," it's like swimming in a pool full of crystal clear water. However, when you're in contact with icky feeling energy or clutter, it feels as if someone has just dumped a wheelbarrow full of dirt into your pool! You just want to get out of the murky or muddy feeling and get it off your being.

Tips To Clear Murky Energy:

1) Keep your house, car, and workspace clear of clutter. It's unrealistic that you'll be able to do this all of the time, but try and make sure things get organized and cleaned at least weekly.

2) Dust! Dust holds a lot of murky energy, so if you don't want to dust, hire someone to do it for you because it's important.

3) Burn incense or sage. Incense is really great and sandle-wood is one of the best to burn when clearing your space. You should burn incense after cleaning. It's a good idea to walk all the way through your house, walking the perimeter with it first, then place it on the counter or the table to finish clearing the energy.

4) Clean with soap and water. Wipe down counters and surfaces with water and a small bit of soap. Also, whenever you feel like you've picked up this murky energy from somewhere and you can feel it on your hands or your entire being, make sure to wash your hands or take a shower. The minute you wash yourself off with water, you should feel better. If not, then it wasn't murky energy in the first place.

What most people probably think of when hearing about clairtangency is the ability to handle an object or touch an area and perceive through your hands to obtain psy-chic knowledge about the article, its owner, or history. It's the ability to hold an item in your hand and essentially give a "reading" about this particular item. If you'd like to learn how to develop and utilize your psychic sense in this manner, refer to Psychic Senses Partner Exercise #2 in the chapter, "What Are Your Psychic Senses?" It's covered under the "objects" exercise.

Clairgustance (Clear Tasting) and Clairscent (Clear Smelling)

Clairgustance is an extrasensory perception that allegedly allows you to taste a substance without putting anything in your mouth. Those who possess this ability are able to obtain psychic knowledge through taste.

Clairscent is where a person acquires psychic knowledge primarily by means of smelling.

These two are very, very similar, and they are the least common among all of the psychic senses. These senses are used for spirit communication.

It's common for a spirit to try and help you tune into their presence via taste or smell. For instance, you may have experienced at some point in your life, catching a brief scent of a cigar, a flower, or perfume with no reasonable explanation why. Or you may have experienced tasting something distinct and specific such as wine, pizza, or fruit, without having eaten it in the first place, causing some bewilderment. When experiencing clairgustance or clairscent, these tastes and smells will occur in the physical absence of that particular item. They may come at a time when you find yourself thinking about a loved one who has passed over. Sometimes, however, the scent or taste may appear simultaneously with a vision or mental picture of someone who is in the spirit realm.

I'll tell you an experience I had with both of these psychic senses. I was at home alone one afternoon, not doing much, when I could sense a spirit in my area. This isn't an uncommon occurrence for me, in fact, it happens quite often. So I did what I usually do when I'm not working ... I ignored it! Because of the psychic work and mediumship I do, I have many spirits trying to contact me before readings or when they want me to tell a loved one something, but if I paid attention every time it happened, I would never be able to live my own life. So I went on about my business. This spirit was rather persistent, however, and the next thing I knew, I could smell cigar smoke. It was so strong for a minute that it compelled me to glance around and see where it was coming from, only to quickly remember I was alone in the house. When I made that connection, I could feel the pleased spirit. However, still off the clock, I went right back to ignoring it. I've had many experiences when I've come in contact with scents when spirits where present, so it only grabbed my attention for a minute or two. Then all of a sudden, I had the most overpowering taste of whisky in my mouth! It was one of the top ten most bizarre experiences I've ever had when encountering a spirit. Especially since I drink alcohol maybe twice a year, and I really hate the taste of whisky! I hate to admit it, but up until this point, I was even a little bit skeptical about this whole clairgustance ability, as I had yet to experience it myself. But I must say, that made me a believer instantly! I could no longer ignore this spirit, so I said, "All right, you got my attention." Turns out when I tuned into this particular spirit, it was my husband's great uncle, who had passed. He was very close to our family and my husband, so I was grateful for his persistence.

Like I mentioned earlier, people who communicate often with spirits are primarily the ones who will utilize these two abilities. So don't be disappointed if you've never experienced either of these psychic senses. I've been working with spirits for more than twenty years and I've only experienced these two things a handful of times. If this psychic sense is available to you, great! If not, don't worry about it.

Everyone is born with their own "sixth sense," however, some people have different abilities than others, and many people have advanced their own abilities to varying degrees. It's kind of like being an athlete; most of us are born with the ability to participate in sports. In fact, it's really important for you to exercise to stay physically healthy. And with training, we can become really good at whatever sport we enjoy. However, some people are born with the natural ability to play football, others to play soccer; some even at the professional level if they choose to do so. It's the same thing with your psychic senses and psychic ability. Some people are born with the natural ability to be clairvoyant, clairaudient, claircognizant, be an empath, or even to become a professional psychic or medium. Using one or two of these senses versus using all of them doesn't determine one's ability. You may have a person who uses only one or two of the psychic senses who has a much stronger ability than someone who uses four. If you're experiencing some of your own psychic abilities, you can work on fine-tuning them more when you understand how you've acquired it. This can take some practice, so look at it like baseball. Even with practice it can sometimes be frustrating, but there's nothing like the feeling you get when the hard work pays off and you hit a home run!

Dreaming and Psychic Ability

Here's an area which is greatly overlooked when it comes to developing psychic ability. Dreaming is actually one of the easiest, most natural ways to connect with the spirit world and utilize your psychic senses. For over fifty years, scientists have continued to study the science behind dreaming. The only really solid reason they have come up with for the reason behind why we dream is because we get sleepy! It's had scientists baffled for years, and will continue to do so, as they aren't looking for the answers they're seeking in the right place. They've failed to study dreaming/sleeping from a spiritual aspect, as they are scientists, studying from the physical side. From a physical perspective, they have proven we get enough rest during the day from sitting at our desks, driving our cars, and sitting while watching TV, that sleep is not required for our physical body.

It is, however, required for our spiritual health. We've been programmed through our Soul DNA, or spiritual genetic system, to spiritually align ourselves every single day, and it's called sleep.

What is spiritual alignment?

It's a time in which we break away from the physical realm and its limitations to explore other dimensions, other realities, and become spiritually free with no limitations.

We astral travel, we have complete access to the spirit world, we tap into our psychic abilities, and we reach higher consciousness. It is, and should be viewed as an extension of your reality. Nowadays, you're told from a very young age your dreams are like a fantasy, or something that doesn't exist. Eventually, you start to believe this information as fact, that dreaming isn't a reality, which could not be further from the truth …

For the last five hundred years or so, dreaming has very much been viewed as useless; it's just something you do each night as a break from real life. But it hasn't always been this way. In fact, it used to be very different.

Dreaming has been embraced a lot more throughout history than it is today. Dreaming is taken for granted in the modern world, mostly because of people's lack of understanding, and the knowledge behind why we dream having been lost and/or forgotten. Ancient civilizations had a great understanding of why we dream, and they used to revolve their everyday lives around what they would see in their dreams. In fact, it was very important in helping them function. Dreams were found recorded on clay tablets dating back to around 4000–3000 BC. Ancient civilizations didn't see dreaming as something they did while asleep, they actually saw it as an extension of their reality. They didn't try and separate the differences between real life and dreaming, but instead molded them together as one and lived their lives this way. Romans and Greeks are great examples of how big an impact dreams had on their lives. They believed dreams were direct messages from the Gods, forewarning them about future events, or advice and guidance on what they should do. It was highly encouraged by most religions to listen to your dreams. They would not only listen to their dreams, but they would look to them for guidance. They'd look into their dreams for answers to problems they were having. For example, before technology was invented to help diagnose a sickness, or help determine what medicine you should take, people would instead look to their dreams for answers on what was wrong with them, and how to heal themselves.

There were also dream analysts people could go to if they didn't understand their dreams. The dream analysts would analyze the dream for you and give you the messages behind your dreams. Dream analysts were looked up to and highly respected. They were usually a big part of the decision making process for the government or the military. Military leaders would use them to help with tactics in order to defeat their enemies. In the Hellenistic times in Greece, they built temples called Asclepieions, where sick people would go and sleep, and the cures would be given to them via dreams.

Ancient Chinese and Mexican civilizations believed that your spirit would actually leave your body while you were dreaming and would wander to other places. They believed if you were to awaken while your body was in a deep sleep, and your spirit was wandering, it would not find its way back to the body, and you would die. Some cultures still look down upon alarm clocks, for fear of suddenly being woken up. They also believed they were able to speak to their ancestors through their dreams, and that their ancestors were made up of different objects or parts of nature in the dreams, but their spirit was in them. As you can see, dreams had a huge impact on people's lives back in history, and many of them had the same theory of being guided and warned of events in the waking life. However, dreaming was not always looked at as something positive. During the Middle Ages, people looked at dreams as horrible tricks. People believed that while you where dreaming, the devil was tempting you with certain images and temptations in your most vulnerable state. Therefore, they did not embrace dreams, and basically had the exact opposite understanding of them than more ancient civilizations. In modern times, scientists started doing tests on the brain and body while people were in a dreaming state and found there's a lot more brain activity going on than when you're awake.

Now it seems people are so sidetracked by technology and materials that they've lost interest in one of the most amazing abilities they have: the ability to spiritually align yourself and shift dimensions while being able to maintain a physical existence!

Now that you have a better understanding of what dreaming actually is — an extension of your reality — and that it naturally allows you to tap into your psychic abilities while also allowing you very easy access into the spirit world, I'm going to give you another exercise. I'm sure you've heard of this exercise before, it's called dream journaling.

Dream Journaling

Why dream journaling? Because this is the first step in helping you remember your dreams, even if you don't think you dream. Secondly, it will allow you to become more familiar with this "other reality" and the other dimensions that you visit. When you become more aware of these things, and you realize on a waking consciousness level that other realities exist and other experiences with the consciousness are possible, then you activate certain potentials within yourself. It alters electromagnetic connections both within the mind, brain, and even perceptive mechanisms. These things will then bring together reservoirs of energy, allowing the waking conscious mind to increase its sensitivity. This allows you to no longer be afraid of other realities, which is a huge step in letting your resistance down in order to develop your psychic senses. Lastly, it helps you to learn how to analyze what information you're receiving from the spirit world or your Spirit Guides. You're very susceptible to receiving valid information during your dream state, as you have just learned from our little history lesson.

1) First you should pick a good dream journal and leave it by your bed. Pick something that you like, try not to just throw a few sheets of paper over there, unless that's all you have at the moment. A journal specifically picked to be your dream journal helps to keep everything in order and not be cluttered with other things like shopping lists, etcetera. Also, make sure you have something to write with. I don't want you searching around for something to write with in the morning.

2) This is very ***important:*** always write in your dream journal first thing in the morning. You're still in a groggy state when you wake up, and you're still tapped into your higher consciousness, so this is when you can really get some great information. The later in the day it gets, the foggier the dream becomes and it makes it very hard to remember all of the details.

3) Try to write something in your dream journal every day for two months, even if it's something short that seems insignificant. Often, writing will jog your memory of other things that happened during the dream state. These two months are also important because you are honing this new skill.

4) Ask for guidance before you fall asleep. Talk to your Spirit Guide and ask them for their guidance. Ask them

to help you with a specific problem at work, a personal issue, or whatever it is you're stressed about. Don't get frustrated if you don't "dream" your solution right away. This is a training process; you're shifting your perspective on why you dream, and training yourself to utilize dreaming more effectively. This takes time. Your belief system has been in place for many, many years, with the perspective that dreaming was not even useful. This belief has allowed many people to block dreaming from their memory, as insignificant to their life. When you realize it actually is an extension of your reality with the potential to help you to receive much needed guidance, it can also be a little bit of added pressure.

5) Give each dream a name or title. This helps you to find dreams faster if you're searching for a specific one later. It also allows you to sum up the over all "feel" of the experience you are going to be writing down. It's like giving a title to a story. Sometimes just naming the dream or giving it a title can trigger an awareness of the overall meaning of the dream.

6) Put more emphasis on the "feel" of the dream than the actual dream itself. Write down symbols and all of that, but make sure you note how you felt throughout the dream; lost, confused, happy, concerned, etcetera. This theme on how you "feel" is repetitive when developing your spirit communication skills. Your sixth sense is felt in the body, and throughout this entire process you are going to retrain

yourself how to get back in touch with these senses. So, in essence, how you "feel" during the dream is just as important as everything else you can remember.

7) After writing down your dream, look at your dream from an outsider's perspective View it from outside of yourself and try and form an overall picture of what the dream means with no attachment. Try and connect the dots; if you're scared of something and you dream about it, then you're probably facing something during your waking conscious state that you're scared of. For instance, I used to be scared of tornados, so when I was really stressed out, I would dream about them. If I was just a little stressed, I would dream about one or two tornados. However, if I was really stressed out, I would dream about six or seven of them, each one representing something different. When I dream about where I am on my life path, I'll dream about roads, such as where I am on the road, if I'm lost on the road, etcetera.

If you do this exercise for a while, slowly you'll be able to receive psychic information via dreaming. However, like I mentioned before, be persistent and patient. I worked on this for about a year before I got really, really good at it.

Grounding Yourself

One of the most important things to learn when working with your psychic senses is grounding.

What is grounding?

Grounding is ridding yourself of excess "psychic" energy, which your spiritual body has picked up externally, and replenishing your physical body with energy from the earth, which is more of a "physically" based energy.

It's essentially bringing your spiritual and physical bodies back into balance with one another, by balancing both energies.

Your physical body and your spiritual body both pick up and "hold" different types of energies: physical energies and spiritual energies. Imagine your body is like a boat floating on the water, and each half of the boat represents a different body. The front of the boat represents your spiritual body and the back of the boat represents your physical body. Imagine for a minute that whenever you stop at a port, you picked up some "excess stuff" in the form of very heavy boxes. But instead of paying attention to the effect this "excess stuff" has on the boat, you just placed them all on the front of the boat each time you came into a port. If you continued to do this, what would eventually happen? Your boat would become so off balance it would become hard to operate, or it may even potentially sink! The same thing would also happen if you placed all of the boxes on the back end of the boat. The best solution is to keep the boat in balance, and to distribute the "excess stuff" more evenly. It would also be a good idea to even rid your boat of excess stuff, stuff that you don't need, at each port. This allows your boat to stay evenly balanced, in good operation, and "free of excess stuff" which is no longer needed.

That's what grounding does for you and your bodies, it frees you of "excess stuff" (or energies), which you pick up along the way, and makes sure you have a balance of both energies.

So how can you tell if you need to be grounded? You'll feel like you have too much excess stuff or energy attached to you, or you'll feel depleted of energy.

You Need To Ground Yourself If:

- You feel shaky or weak after being around a person or a group of people.

- You spend so much time using your psychic senses that you no longer feel "present."
- You feel "out of body."

These things can be really annoying, but it's what happens when your physical energies and spiritual energies are no longer in balance. These things can also occur when you're doing a lot of spiritual work. When I really started to develop my psychic senses, I used to hate it when I would begin to feel "out of body" or "not present." I would feel as if I was watching my life on a movie screen! I'd get in my car to drive somewhere and I'd feel completely disconnected from my physical body. The bad part was, I didn't even know what was causing it, or what to do about it at the time. No one knew what I was talking about, which freaked me out even more.

Now, however, my energy is much stronger. It still happens to me on occasion, especially when I do psychic events. These are times when I'm doing readings for 10 hours straight. Talk about needing to be grounded! So I meditate before I go, make sure I drink water the whole time I'm there, take a hot shower (with scented shower gel) after, and burn incense before going to bed. I have a routine for myself, and it works really well. You should too when you're working with your psychic senses.

Here are some helpful grounding techniques:

Eight Ways To Ground Yourself

1) Meditation.

Meditation is a very easy way to ground yourself. If you don't know what kind of meditation to do … well, any kind works, really. But for those of you who'd like to use a special grounding meditation, I have included one at the end of this chapter.

2) Through scents.

Burning incense is one of the most common ways to ground yourself using scents. Sandlewood is one of the most popular and effective grounding incenses to use. However, you can also use scented soaps in the shower, perfumes, oils, and even lotions. Some scents work faster than others. I find flower type smells will not ground you nearly as fast as musk type smells.

3) Drinking water.

Drinking plenty of water is very important when you're working with your psychic senses. If you need grounding, drink water and stay away from sugar drinks. Not forever, just until you feel more balanced. I love sugar drinks as much as the next person (well, probably more), but I only drink water when I'm doing psychic work for a long period of time.

4) Exercise.

Again, I'm not trying to make you all healthy or anything, but exercise is really important when you're working with your psychic senses. It keeps you connected with your physical body. It helps immensely with keeping you in balance.

5) Nature.

Go outside and just "be" in nature. Or do anything that has to do with Mother Earth, such as planting, gardening, or hiking. Take your shoes off and walk on the ground. Anything that has nature (plants, dirt, sand, or rocks) coming into contact with your skin (hands or feet) is perfect!

6) Yoga.

Yoga is specifically designed to align your spiritual and physical bodies! Take a yoga class, or do yoga on your own with a DVD.

7) Chocolate.

Yes, ladies, I'm not kidding! Eat chocolate when you feel you need to be grounded. Dark chocolate is the best (although I'm not sure why), but any chocolate will work. So eat chocolate for the sake of staying balanced!

8) Sex

Sex is a very physical act, and therefore, it's very grounding to your physical body. It really heightens your physical senses and allows you to become very aware of your physical body, which helps you to become grounded again.

Grounding is all about getting yourself back in touch with your physical body.

Grounding Meditation Exercise

This meditation exercise is designed to specifically help ground yourself. It's a very effective exercise, which should be done at least once a day. It's especially helpful when you're stressed out, around a bunch of people, or have been exposed to negative energy of any kind.

1) Find a quiet place where you will not be disturbed.

2) Sit comfortably in a chair or in an upright position. Hands to your side and feet flat on the floor. Don't cross your hands, feet, or legs.

3) Close your eyes and concentrate on your breathing. Slow your breathing to a relaxed state.

4) When your breathing is rhythmic, concentrate on relaxing all of the muscles in your body.

5) Imagine your spine is like a string on a musical instrument. Imagine that this string or cord attaches all of your chakras together, from your root chakra (base of your spine) to your crown chakra (top of your head).

6) Visualize this string or cord vibrating. Imagine you are in control of how fast or slow the vibration is. Next raise this vibration to the highest level of vibration you can achieve.

7) When you're vibrating at a high level, imagine a red beam of light comes from above your body, through the top of your head, and down your spine. Feel it travel slowly through each of your chakras. Then imagine the red beam continues out through the bottom of your tailbone, through the chair, into the earth. See the light go deep, deep into the earth until it reaches the middle. When it reaches the center of the earth, imagine you anchor the red beam to the earth.

8) Next, visualize all of the extra energy you've picked up from places you've been and the people you've seen throughout the day. See this energy naturally flowing down this light into the earth, almost as if you had rolled in dirt and you're now taking a shower. Feel the energy flow down the drain (the red beam of light), feel how clean your energetic being is becoming as this extra energy (that does not belong to you), is released into the earth.

9) See and "feel" this energy becoming absorbed into the earth. Let the natural flow continue until you feel completely clean, and free of any energetic residue. Take a moment to bask in the clean feeling of your energetic being, enjoy how that feels.

10) Next, imagine a white light coming from the middle of Mother Earth, coming up through the ground, to your chair, gently coming up through your root chakra, continuing to touch each chakra as it travels to the top of your head. This white light is recharging your energetic field with new energy from Mother Earth, replacing any of your own energy you have lost throughout the day. Feel this energy recharging your system as it fills each chakra and continues up the spine, and out through the top of your head.

11) Each time this new energy moves through a chakra, imagine that it disperses energy to other parts of the body. Feel the energy disperse, kind of like when you watch fireworks explode. You can do this as long as you like.

12) Remain in this state until you feel a sense of completion, then release this image into the Universe.

I like to do this every morning, although many people enjoy doing this exercise at night. There's no right or wrong as to the time you spend, you should adjust the time to whatever feels right to you.

BONUS CHAPTERS

The "Real Power" Behind Pendulums

I have a very strong opinion on pendulums, and in my opinion, they should not be used for psychic work—ever! On the flip side, I think pendulums are a very powerful learning tool. So what exactly should they be used for?

To help you to understand the power behind the "Law of Intention."

How does that work? Pendulums can be manipulated by your very own energy ... and it's an amazing thing to witness! Especially when you're the one making the pendulum move. This is why you shouldn't ever use pendulums to help you find the answer to a question. Especially if you're trying to get an answer by watching the way in which it moves or spins. Because you can manipulate pendulums, you're manipulating your answer.

How do you manipulate a pendulum ...? By using your thoughts or by the "power of intention."

Wow! How cool is that? To have something you can physically see be affected and manipulated by something you cannot see? I've heard you cannot manipulate a crystal or an acrylic pendulum, but you can. I've done it many times and have shown others how to do it to. Frankly, learning how to direct your energy in such a way that you can "feel" your intention is a way more powerful learning tool than having it tell you "yes" or "no" to a question. So I feel that the real power behind the pendulum is extremely underutilized, overlooked, or not even known to most people.

Through this exercise you will experience "the power of thought."

You'll actually experience how it feels when working with the "Law of Intent." You'll really get to see how powerful your thoughts are, and discover how your intent actually has an external effect on the world around you.

Pendulum Exercise

1) Find or make a pendulum. If you don't have one, you can use a light string or piece of thread to attach the pendulum to. For the pendulum, find something weighted, like a screw, bolt, or nut, and attach it to the bottom of the string. I often bring a piece of thread and a screw for my students, as they are common household objects they can find at home.

2) Find a sturdy place to rest your elbow, like a table. Place your elbow on the table and hold the pendulum string between your thumb and pointer finger. Your forearm should make about a 45 degree angle with the table.

3) Hold the pendulum steady with the other hand to initially stop it from swinging. Once the pendulum is still, release it gently.

4) Concentrate on "seeing" the pendulum move in a clockwise circle. As you concentrate on the pendulum, you'll begin to see it move slightly. Keep "seeing it" move in your mind's eye, in a bigger and bigger circle.

5) After the pendulum is moving well clockwise, imagine you now want to "see" the pendulum move in the opposite direction, counter-clockwise. Now visualize and imagine you can make the pendulum move counter-clockwise just by thinking about it and "seeing" it happen. While you're concentrating on moving the pendulum counter-clockwise, you'll see it slowly stop, and it will begin to move in the other direction.

6) Next you can try moving it from side to side, or forward and backward, in the same manner as above.

Practice this and have fun with the exercise. It might start as subtle movements at first, but the more you practice, the better you'll become. You'll learn how to harness and focus your energy. As you learn, you'll begin to move the pendulum with ease, whichever way you choose, faster and faster.

This is a really great exercise which helps train you how to direct your energy properly when it comes to bringing things into your life. It's important to know this is how the power of intent works with energy directed by you in the physical world. It's the same concept when working with the power of intent, which forms things in your future by just imagining them. When you really begin to feel how this works with the pendulum, then you can begin to direct and feel this same energy during meditation while you're working on creating desired outcomes.

This is one of my favorite exercises to teach my students and it's one that absolutely causes the most excitement.

Seven Tips For Helping Intuitive / Psychic Children

While watching a show on television about psychic children, I thought back to my own childhood and remembered how frightening it could be. I would watch all of these children trying to learn how to deal with their abilities and it really struck a chord with me.

I thought about my childhood and about how different it was for my own children, what made similar childhoods so different? Where some children are terrified, mine are not. So I started to think about all of the things that I did differently for my own kids. Things that other parents could do. Being psychic or sensitive is not always easy. You are met with skepticism and many times disbelief. People who are not psychic do not understand what you are talking about.

Even as an adult, coming out of the closet as a psychic

wasn't easy. People didn't and still don't always believe I have the gifts and abilities that I have. They don't even stop to think they have some of the same abilities! That's really interesting to me because I don't think I have ever met anyone who hasn't had his or her own "gut" feeling about something, at least once. For me, however, this is my path, and I accept being this way. It's a way of life for me, not something I do for fun.

For my own children, growing up was very different. Since I was already a psychic, my understanding of their gift and my ability to explain to them what it was they were seeing and hearing was very helpful. From the time he was very young, my son would see spirits all over the place. I remember driving by an empty lot one day, where certain people I knew had asked me if they should put up a business there. I told them to look elsewhere, that the vibration and energy weren't good on that lot and it would affect any business that opened up there.

While driving by the empty lot, I asked my son, "What do you see over there?"

He said, "A man in a robe, right there. Oh no, you can't see him anymore. He ran behind that church!"

"What church?" I asked.

He looked back and could no longer see the church. His

eyes grew really big, and he exclaimed, "The church is gone! Why did I see that?"

I told him he was seeing an old church that had been there years ago, and the monk was in the same time frame as the church. He then added he did not like that area, that it felt weird. His observations were correct. There was an energy imprint on that piece of property, and a lot of strange things had happened there over the years, which has not helped to improve the area.

My kids have grown up knowing the spirits they see are real, and there's nothing for them to be scared of because they cannot hurt them in any way. We are spiritual beings. We've always had a lot of spirits around and about the homes in which we've lived. My kids and I always talked about the spirits that are in our houses, even the mischievous ones. This helped my children understand they're a part of life. When my son was little, he used to say, "I feel sorry for people who don't have spirits around. It must feel lonely." I agree … I like feeling them around, too.

Knowledge is very important. If you don't know the answers to your children's questions, buy a book or talk with someone who might know the answer. Let them know that all of their questions are good ones. For you and your children, knowledge is power!

Seven Tips For Helping Intuitive/Psychic Children:

Here are some easy things I put together to help you with psychic children. My son and daughter are very well-adjusted kids. They don't live in fear of their abilities; they live in harmony with them. This information can help intuitive children live basically "normal" lives without fear:

1) Realize that because your child is psychic, it doesn't mean he or she is meant to become a professional psychic.

The majority of children have psychic abilities, this ability most likely will not determine their career path. It's meant to be a guidance system. (This is not the path my children will take.)

2) It's important to make sure your children understand what their ability is.

It's good for them to know if they're an empath, what an empath is, etcetera. Also, their gifts and abilities are real and will most likely always be a part of their everyday life. You want to teach them how to live in harmony with their abilities and be comfortable with them. However, in time they can learn, to some extent, how to tune it out.

3) Make sure your children know spirits will not harm them!

It's hard for psychics and intuitives to sleep at night without hearing all kinds of spiritual racket. Keeping the television on helped my son to sleep. (I highly recommend this with sensitive children.) Allow them to listen to SpongeBob or whatever is uplifting and light. I've had parents say, "I'm afraid if I do that, they won't sleep!" I promise you, if they're sensitive, they're probably not sleeping now. This trick allows them to drift right into a heavy sleep, much more important than no sleep at all. I do this myself most nights; it drowns out the noise and gives my mind something else to listen to. Spirits are active at night, and our minds are very receptive when we're going to sleep. It's like opening the floodgates to the Other Side.

4) Your children should learn psychic protection.

Being psychic can be energetically draining. Your children should learn psychic protection. If they're not paying attention, they pick up on other people's energy and take on their emotions without realizing it. This can happen anywhere, especially in a crowded area such as a mall or at school. If this is a problem, have them imagine themselves in a bubble surrounded by a white light that doesn't allow another's energy to get through. Then have them ask God to dissolve other people's energy into the white light of the Holy Spirit. Teach them the Bubble Protection that is found earlier in this book. Have them do this before you go somewhere crowded. Taking on everyone else's feelings can make them feel anxious, especially somewhere like a department store. They can also just choose not to be affected by this. If they recognize that these feelings are not their own, they can tell their body that they are calm and healthy. They can decide they won't allow another person's emotions to make them feel any differently. They have control over their own body!

5) It's also important to pay attention to what your children say and to take them seriously.

Don't disregard what they're saying because they're young. For instance, if they don't like someone or they're uncomfortable with a specific situation, there's usually a very valid reason. Children can sense someone's energy and intentions like nobody's business.

6) You need to let your children know they're in total control of their abilities.

Sometimes when you're in tune with your psychic abilities, there's a feeling of having no control over what you're experiencing. You can ask not to be shown things you can't do anything about or that you have no control over. For instance, it was very scary when I was younger and knew my little brother was going to be in a car accident. I had no control over this; and I just had to wait and pray he would be okay. Luckily, as he drove his car into a ravine, it happened to land on the only pile of trees in that area. This barely kept his car from launching over the hill several hundred feet to the bottom. I asked not to be shown these things I have no control over, and haven't had this sort of problem since.

7) Decide if and when to let others know about their abilities.

I discussed with my children that their friends and the parents of their friends may have a hard time understanding their gifts. I left it up to them to let their friends know about their abilities or mine. Remember, your child is psychic; you need to trust his or her judgment.

The Ten Commandments of Seeing a Psychic

Okay, I'm hearing way too many stories of people seeing bad psychics! Here's the thing, there are a lot, and I mean a lot, of bad psychics out there. In fact, I'd say that out of every ten psychics, eight shouldn't be giving psychic readings. I'm not saying these psychics are evil or just trying to take your money. I'm just saying that even if their intent is good, they're not developed enough to be giving psychic readings to other people. Just because you're psychic, it doesn't mean you can do readings ... that's a whole different ball game. You must have training and a mentor in most cases, which many do not, and years of experience under your belt. How do I know this? Because I've been in the industry for over twenty years, I've been around other psychics my whole life and I personally have been read by five! Why? Since I've been in this industry for so long, I'm very particular about who gives me a reading, because I know what's out there.

I also don't want you to be afraid of getting a psychic reading either, so I've put together a list that will help you.

The Ten Commandments of Seeing a Psychic

1) Thou shalt not take the psychic's word as the "law of the land." God gave us free will — use it!

2) Thou shalt not see a psychic more than once every three months (only on rare occasions). We then resort to having to tell you things like "I see you getting some new shoes." Let's face it, life doesn't change that quickly!

3) Thou shalt not push our own intuition aside, or stop relying on it.

4) Thou shalt not remove clothes or be touched for a reading (unless you're having your palm read). If this is the only way you can get a reading, find another psychic!

5) Thou shalt use the psychic reading as advice or guidance.

6) Thou shalt realize that no psychic is 100% accurate, therefore refer to #3 and #5.

7) Thou shalt never replace a physician, financial planner, or lawyer with a psychic. These are specialists trained in a specific area. Most psychics are specialized in spiritual areas and life coaching.

8) Thou shalt use psychics and mediums for insight with spiritual issues, life path, and loved ones passing on.

9) Thou shalt use psychics to verify or clarify your own intuition. Psychics can be great teachers to help you learn how to become more in tune with your own psychic ability and develop it.

10) Thou shalt trust your gut when meeting a psychic for the first time. Don't hesitate to change your mind if you're not comfortable. All psychics are different and you should look until you find one you are comfortable with. (Golden Rule)

When you have a psychic reading, it should be an overall positive experience. The best in the industry can see things you should avoid or be aware of and guide you towards a better outcome. If you are left feeling:

Scared
Worried
Upset
With a stomach ache

Disregard the reading, and don't go back! These are all signs of having had a **Bad Psychic Reading!** And if they try to get you to pay them money to break or rid yourself of a curse, red flag! Not a psychic, but a con artist. Shop around, get a referral, read their books, or listen to their radio show until you get a sense of them. You can usually tell right away, just use your own intuition and never forget, **#10 is the Golden Rule!**

BONUS

Two Chapters from Energy Vampires:

What Is An Energy Vampire?

You've probably heard the term "energy vampires" before, especially if you're at all interested in psychic ability or psychic development. But what exactly are energy vampires? They're not real vampires. Well, I guess they're real vampires, but not like the ones you see in Twilight … "Energy vampires" feed upon your energy. In other words, their primary target is your spiritual body, not your physical body.

"Energy vampires" are people who constantly draw upon other people's energy in order to help "recharge" their own system.

So what do energy vampires and negative people have in common?

They essentially do the same thing. They draw upon your energy, and they will have a very profound effect on your system, both spiritually and physically. Many times, they will wear you down to the point of exhaustion. However, unless you're aware of what is happening, you may not even notice the effects these people are having in your life, on a day-to-day basis. You may just think you've had a hard day and that's why you feel so exhausted, or you may think you're just more tired than usual, but you don't know why. People don't usually think, "Maybe it's the people I'm around." In fact, for many people, this is the furthest thought from their mind. Their mind tends to relate this "drained" feeling to their job, or stress they're under at home. But think about it, what's the worst part about your job? Dealing with your boss? Dealing with impossible coworkers? Dealing with unreasonable customers? All of these stressors involve people! What about stress in your life? Many times, stress you're under in life tends to involve your friends, husband, wife, kids, parents, and people who just make you mad. More people!

So who exactly do energy vampires and negative people affect?

Simple … Everybody!

You don't need to be a healer, energy worker, or a psychic for energy vampires and negative people to have a very profound effect on you, or on your life. Everybody is susceptible to experiencing the after effects of being around energy vampires and negative people. It has the same spiritual and physical side effects; some people just don't realize what's happening to them. They just think being tired is a part of life ... a part of being a grown up! They think being exhausted is what everybody feels like most of time. They don't realize this isn't always how you're supposed to feel. You shouldn't feel tired most of the time. You should feel good most of the time, and tired only some of the time. If you're tired most of the time, this is a very good book for you.

Awareness Is Key

There are certain things which you can do and be aware of when dealing with "energy vampires" in order to help minimize the effect they have on your life.

These things also tend to be the same things you would do when dealing with negative people in your life, since they essentially fall into the same category, so from this point on you can use energy vampires and negative people interchangeably.

Why are some people more aware of energy vampires than others? Some of you may even be wondering, "Why have I never noticed them before, but now I do?"

People who decide they want to make a change in their life tend to become acutely aware of the negative people in their life.

Imagine it like *Star Wars*; you can feel the force of the dark side. The more you decide to enlighten yourself, become more positive, or to enhance your spirituality, the more the dark side, or negativity, will become apparent on your radar. Why? Because doing all these things will help you align yourself spiritually. It helps you to raise your vibration and become more balanced spiritually and physically. When this happens, negativity will bother you more then it ever did before, even when your circumstances haven't changed and the same people have been in your life for many years. You've changed, and you're becoming more spiritually aware.

For instance, ask yourself these things:

1) Are you learning what it's like to be more positive?
2) Are you learning how to change your life for the better?
3) Are you on a new spiritual journey?
4) Are you learning how to develop your psychic senses?
5) Are you noticing more and more that negative people surround you?

With this new consciousness era, there is an energetic shift beginning to take place, and many people are beginning to feel their spiritual bodies awaken. Where they were only aware of their physical body before, this is beginning to change. They can feel this shift taking place, and people are beginning to crave spiritual growth. In attempts to help awaken and connect their spiritual and physical bodies (even though they may not be fully aware of what is happening), they embark on a new spiritual journey, figuring out how to change their lives for the better. However, one thing that begins to trip them up is they no longer know how to handle the negative people in their lives. Whereas these people never seemed to bother them so much in the past, they're now having a different effect on them. It seems to bother them, it makes them a little uncomfortable. So how do you cope with them? How do you keep them in your life and still stay positive, especially, since many times, these people are close friends and family?

This adverse reaction to negativity is new to many people. When you're not sure what to do, or how to deal with negativity, it makes this new journey harder than it has to be.

Another thing happening during this new spiritual awakening is many people are discovering they are empaths. Do you have to be an empath in order to have energy vampires or negative people affect you? No. In fact, you just have to be ... well, human. But it's helpful to know if you are an empath, because empaths are way more sensitive to energy vampires and negative people than most other people. Because of this I have devoted a chapter in my book *Energy Vampires* to empaths.

This is the end of the sample of Energy Vampires. Buy the book to learn about empaths and more.

One of the best "Vampire Books" you will ever read!

Especially if you are surrounded by negative thinking or negative people...

After being around certain people do you ever find youself feeling:

- Emotionally exhausted
- Drained
- Tired or wanting to take a nap?

If so, then this is a good book for you!

Who exactly do energy vampires and negative people affect?

Simple ... Everybody!

So what is an energy vampire? You've probably heard the term "energy vampires" before, especially if you're at all interested in psychic ability or psychic development. But what exactly are energy vampires? They're not real vampires. Well, I guess they're real vampires, but not like the ones you see in Twilight ... "Energy vampires" feed upon your energy. In other words, their primary target is your spiritual body, not your physical body.

"Energy vampires" are people who constantly draw upon other people's energy in order to help "recharge" their own system.

So what do energy vampires and negative people have in common?

They essentially do the same thing. They draw upon your energy, and they will have a very profound effect on your system, both spiritually and physically. Many times, they will wear you down to the point of exhaustion. However, unless you're aware of what is happening, you may not even notice the effects these people are having in your life, on a day-to-day basis.

Empaths, this is the book for you!

Empaths and sensitives are very susceptible to "energy vampires" more so than most other people. More and more people are discovering they are empaths in this new consciousness area. You may even be one and never knew it, until now. How do you find out if you are an empath? By reading this book!

In The Book Find Out:

- How to spot an "energy vampire"
- How to protect yourself against negativity

- What to do if you if you are surrounded by negative people
- How to tell if you are an empath!
- How to protect yourself if you are an empath
- What effects "energy vampires" have on your spiritual and physical health
- How to live in a world filled with "energy vampires"
- And the very important...energy vampire first aid!

Author Bio:

Spiritual teacher and best selling author Jennifer O'Neill is devoted to helping others learn how to live a happier life through her books, readings and workshops. The focus of her writing and teaching is to simplify the process of using the spiritual tools and gifts you were born with in a way that fits into your everyday life.

Jennifer is also one of Hawaii's top psychics and the leading expert in the field of Soul DNA and the originator of the Soul DNA© process. She has spent the last twenty years as a professional psychic and spiritual teacher helping people all over the world with their spiritual growth.

You can find information on Jennifer's radio show, blog, books and workshops on her website www.hawaiihealings.com.

Updates on other books: www.limitlesspublishing.com

Made in the USA
Coppell, TX
24 July 2021